Confessions of a Cancer-Fighting Wife

Finding God's Strength in the Tender and Trying Moments of Cancer, Caregiving, and Grief

Alisa Cochrane

Preacher's Hill Publishing

This book is intended to provide encouragement and personal reflection from the author's experience. It is not intended as medical, legal, or professional advice. Readers should consult appropriate professionals where needed. The author and publisher assume no liability for any actions taken in reliance on the information contained herein.

ISBN: 979-8-218-86867-3
Printed in the United States of America
First Edition, 2025

Cover design by Wes Connell
Interior design by Preacher's Hill Publishing

Photo Credits:
Author photo by Erica Campbell Photography
Doug and Spot photo courtesy of Alisa Cochrane

Author Website: www.alisacochrane.com

Dedication

To my beloved husband, Doug,
who walked courageously through the cancer journey.
Your faith, strength, and love continue to inspire me.

And to all the wives who faithfully walk beside their husbands in
the fight against cancer, may you find comfort, courage, and peace
in God's presence.

Contents

Hello Sunshine   1

Confessions of Hope   4

Confessions of Faith   22

Confessions of Depression   40

Confessions of Grace   57

Confessions of Fear and Despair   69

Confessions of Courage   91

Confessions of Health and Healing   108

Confessions of Grief   124

In the Quiet Place: Pages of Hope and Healing   140

Afterword — A Letter from My Heart   175

Acknowlegments   177

About the Author   178

Scripture References   179

Hello Sunshine

I am a survivor of the sacred, yet difficult, work of caregiving for a loved one with cancer, and if you are reading this, you may be as well.

In May of 2021, my husband, Doug, was diagnosed with stage 4 lung cancer. From that moment, our lives were forever changed. For thirty-eight months, he fought the disease valiantly, and I stood by his side every step of the way. Together, we experienced the highs and lows of the cancer journey—moments of hope, moments of fear, and seasons of deep weariness.

Yet through it all, God was with us. His presence carried us through the darkest nights and reminded us that peace could be found even in the midst of a storm. Doug and I discovered that courage doesn't come from our own strength, but from trusting God to hold us, guide us, and sustain us.

As a wife and caregiver, I have learned that it is essential to be honest about the emotions that accompany this role. Fear, sadness, grief, and even depression are not signs of weakness; they are part of the human heart responding to suffering. God knows us intimately—He sees the tears we cry in secret, hears the prayers we cannot put into words, and understands the weight we carry daily as we care for our husbands. And just as He sees our sorrow, He also offers us His comfort, His promises, and His unfailing love.

This devotional was written with the guidance of the Holy Spirit to offer encouragement to wives navigating the challenging path of caregiving. My prayer is that, through these words, you will be reminded that you are not alone. God is with you, strengthening you, and tenderly caring for you, even as you pour yourself out for the one you love.

A FEW MORE WORDS...

I've included **declarations**, **prayers of reflection**, and **journal prompts** throughout this devotional to make it a true resource for you as you walk this sacred journey of caregiving.

The Word says, '*Death and life are in the power of the tongue*' (Proverbs 18:21). Our words can build up or tear down—not only others, but ourselves. They bring encouragement and healing when they speak life, but can cause fear and defeat when negative. As caregivers, our words shape our days and our home's atmosphere. An evangelist once said, '*Our words create our world,*' and I've found that true, especially in caregiving.

When we speak **positive declarations**, we strengthen our spirit and change our minds. Science shows that words of life can rewire the brain, sparking peace, motivation, and joy. Speaking faith-filled declarations lowers stress, reduces cortisol, and builds resilience. Most importantly, it helps us see hope over despair. Make speaking life a daily habit—it works!

Through the **prayers of reflection**, my hope is that you will find connection and encouragement. I invite you to personalize them—insert your name and the name of your loved one—and use them as a framework for your own heartfelt prayers. Let these prayers become intimate conversations between you and God, shaped by your emotions, experiences, and faith.

Throughout my caregiving journey for my husband, Doug, I learned to treasure every moment, no matter the outcome. God met me in both pain and joy. His presence encouraged me in every season, and my prayer is that you are encouraged as well.

And finally, I pray that as you read, write, and reflect, you will feel His peace settle over you. May you be strengthened in spirit and renewed in hope. **Remember: everything will be all right because God is still faithful and His promises never fail.**

In Christ,
Alisa

Confessions of Hope

Rejoice and exult in hope; be steadfast and patient in suffering and tribulation; be constant in prayer. Romans 12:12

"I don't see any cancer at this point. It looks like the treatment was successful. I can confidently say that Doug is in remission. We don't use the word 'cancer free' until the remission is sustained for at least three years," the radiation oncologist explained as Doug and I stared at the images of his most recent scans displayed on the giant screen in the room.

"Thank You, Jesus!" I exclaimed as tears streamed down my cheeks. Beside me, I heard Doug whisper his own thanks to God. He reached over, took my hand, and in that simple gesture, I felt the depth of our shared relief, gratitude, and hope.

At that moment, we both felt a surge of faith. Against the grim statistics that had been spoken over him, we dared to believe that Doug could walk away as a living testament to God's faithfulness in the midst of suffering and tribulation. It wasn't just about survival—it was about proclaiming that God was present and powerful, even in the valley of cancer.

From that day forward, we anchored ourselves in hope for Doug's complete restoration. We chose joy, even in the little things, and thankfulness in every circumstance. We made a conscious decision to live our lives fully, not in the shadow of fear, but in the light of faith.

That day marked a turning point. We were all in with God—not halfway, not with wavering hearts, but with a renewed determination to trust Him completely. Whatever the outcome, we knew that our story was held in His hands, and we wanted every part of it to reflect His glory.

Say this out loud: **I am steadfast in suffering and constant in prayer.**

Now declare this: **I declare that I will rejoice in hope, remain patient in affliction, and stay faithful in prayer, for my God is with me in every season.**

Paul teaches us to endure hardship with faith. As caregivers or those grieving, we rejoice in hope, knowing God is always at work, even when unseen. We are called to patience in suffering, trusting that it is not the end of our story. We are urged to remain faithful in prayer, which connects us to God's strength when ours fails. This verse shows that hope, patience, and prayer are not just commands, but lifelines in hard seasons.

Prayer of Reflection

Lord, thank You for reminding me that no matter what season I walk through, I can hold onto hope because of You. Teach me to rejoice in the hope of Your promises, even when the road feels dark. Give me patience when affliction weighs heavily and help me to lean into Your timing instead of my own. Keep me faithful in prayer, lifting my heart to You daily, knowing that You hear every word and hold every tear. Strengthen me to trust that You are working all things together for my good. Amen.

Behold, the Lord's eye is upon those who fear Him [who revere and worship Him with awe], who wait for Him and hope in His mercy and loving-kindness. Psalm 33:18

My phone screen told me I had been on hold for fifteen minutes and counting. Frustration started bubbling up as I sat there, waiting for someone—anyone—from the local VA Clinic to answer. Doug was struggling in new and concerning ways. His body no longer seemed able to regulate its temperature. Some days he was chilled to the bone; other days he burned with heat. Deep down, I felt in my spirit that the issue was his thyroid medication.

Doug had just finished several rounds of radiation to his neck and brain, and I suspected the treatments had damaged his thyroid. It seemed clear to me that he was now receiving too much supplementation for low thyroid function. I just needed someone to listen.

Finally, a nurse returned to the line. "Mrs. Cochrane, the doctor on call has reviewed his most recent bloodwork and doesn't see any indication that he needs an adjustment."

I bit my lip. "That bloodwork is almost a month old," I replied carefully. "And since then, he's had several rounds of radiation. Did you tell the doctor that he is currently receiving radiation therapy?" I tried to keep my voice steady and free of frustration, because I had learned the hard way that when dealing with the Department of Veterans Affairs, patience and politeness often got me further than anger ever would.

Her reply was clipped. "No, I did not. He is to stay on his current dose of medication according to the doctor." Her tone carried both finality and exasperation.

I knew at that moment that no amount of arguing would change her mind. So, I thanked her politely and ended the call. But I wasn't finished. My next call was to Doug's private primary care physician, and unlike the VA, I was able to speak with him directly. He listened, reviewed Doug's situation, and agreed that an adjustment was necessary. In time, Doug's medication was modified, and his health began to improve.

That day taught me yet another lesson on our cancer journey: don't take no for an answer when your spouse's health is at stake. Caregiving requires persistence, advocacy, and discernment. There is always a way forward, always another door to knock on, always someone else who might listen. Above all, there is always **HOPE**. Hope that God will guide, provide, and open the right doors even when human systems seem impossible to navigate.

Say this out loud: **I am steadfast in hope.**
Now declare this: **I declare that the Lord's eyes are upon me, and His unfailing love surrounds me because I place my hope in Him.**

God's watchful eye is always on those who revere Him and place their hope in His unfailing love. In times of fear, grief, or uncertainty, we can take comfort in knowing that we are never out of His sight. His care is not distant or passive; it is personal and active, guiding us, protecting us, and surrounding us with steadfast love. When everything else feels fragile, His faithful love becomes the secure foundation on which we can rest.

Prayer of Reflection
Lord, I thank You that Your eyes are always upon me and that Your unfailing love surrounds me. In my grief and in my weakness, I

sometimes feel unseen and forgotten, but this verse reminds me that I am never out of Your sight. You watch over me with tenderness, and You hold my life in Your care.

Teach me to place my hope fully in Your steadfast love rather than in my own strength or circumstances. When fear rises and uncertainty clouds my view, remind me that Your gaze is steady and Your presence is constant. Help me to rest in the assurance that I am cherished, guarded, and guided by You. Amen.

With a view to this we toil and strive, [yes and] suffer re-proach, because we have [fixed our] hope on the living God, Who is the Savior (Preserver, Maintainer, Deliverer) of all men, especially of those who believe (trust in, rely on, and adhere to Him). 1 Timothy 4:10

"We believe in all alternative methods of treatment, including prayer," the radiation oncologist explained after I mentioned that Doug was taking Chinese medicine supplements and consulting with a practitioner in Vermont via telehealth.

"Yes, we believe in prayer," Doug responded with conviction, "and that Jesus is our Healer."

That moment became more than just an exchange; it became a declaration of our faith. This is our promise: if we believe in Him, if we trust Him in our grief and suffering, He will give us hope, and in time, we will realize the victory in our storm.

As believers, we can have confident hope in Christ, the Savior offered for all people. To rest in His love and to hold fast to the blessed assurance that what God says is true makes His promises real and alive in our lives.

From the beginning, Adam and Eve's sin condemned humanity to a fallen, sin-filled world. We live in a culture that celebrates striving, self-sufficiency, and the pursuit of worldly gain. In such a world, choosing instead to rest in God's promises of hope and glory often appears abnormal, even radical. And when we stand steadfast in hope, trusting God to work all things for our good, we may even suffer reproach, scorn, contempt, or disbelief from others.

Yet, it is this very hope that sustains us in our suffering. Without hope, our grief would consume us, harden us, and leave us bitter.

But with hope—living, confident hope in Christ, we discover that suffering becomes a place of transformation. As we surrender our own plans to His, He redeems what feels unbearable. He shapes us into examples of His faithfulness, showing the world that even in loss and hardship, His goodness prevails.

Hope does not deny pain. It does not erase tears. But it does remind us that pain and tears are not the end of the story. Hope is the anchor that keeps us steady, the light that points us forward, and the promise that God Himself preserves, delivers, and carries us through.

Say this out loud: **I am the hope of our living God.**

Now declare this: **I declare that my hope is in the living God, who is my Savior and the faithful Keeper of my life.**

Paul reminds us that our labor and endurance are not in vain because our hope is anchored in the living God. He is the Savior of all who believe, the One who holds our lives securely in His hands. For those navigating caregiving or grief, this verse offers reassurance that our struggles are not meaningless. God sees, God sustains, and God saves. Our perseverance flows from the unshakable hope we have in Him.

Prayer of Reflection

Lord, thank You that in every season of grief and suffering, You remain my living hope. When the weight of illness and loss feels overwhelming, remind me that You are my Healer, my Deliverer, and the Keeper of my soul.

Forgive me for the times I have doubted or tried to carry the burden on my own. Teach me to rest in Your promises, even when the world says it is foolish. Fill me with courage to trust that all things are working together for good, even when I cannot see the outcome.

Let my life be a testimony of steadfast hope—hope that does not deny pain but anchors me in Your love. Preserve me in the storm, deliver me in the valley, and strengthen me to walk forward with confidence that You are faithful, Amen.

For whatever was thus written in former days was written for our instruction, that by [our steadfast and patient] endurance and the encouragement [drawn] from the Scriptures we might hold fast to and cherish hope. Romans 15:4

The Scriptures were given to us for a purpose: to comfort us and to strengthen our patience in the tests and trials of life. And cancer's presence in the body of someone we love is one of the greatest trials we will ever bear.

As caregivers, it is easy to lose ourselves in our spouse's illness. It is easy to take to heart every doctor's report, every grim prediction, until our thoughts begin to spiral and our flesh takes the lead. But in those moments, we must remind ourselves of those who came before us, the lessons of the Old Testament saints, the promises of the New Testament, and the words of Paul that steady our hearts.

Paul reminded the Corinthians that the Scriptures were written for their instruction, to equip them, guide them, and admonish them when they strayed from the path. He warned them not to bow to idols, not to give in to immorality, not to test God's patience by questioning His purposes, and not to murmur in *"unwarranted discontent." (1 Corinthians 10:10)* Those warnings still apply to us today, even in the middle of suffering.

The truth is, our natural human response to something as devastating as cancer is to claim it with our words and wrap our identity in it: *"My husband has cancer. Woe is me."* We speak this way not always out of defiance, but often because our flesh is looking for sympathy, for someone to acknowledge our pain and share our burden. At its root, murmuring is an attempt to connect and be seen. But when discontent becomes our language, it opens the door for bitterness, despair, and even the enemy's lies.

Scripture offers us a better way. Instead of murmuring, we are called to hold fast to God's love and cling to the hope He breathes into our spirits. The Word equips us to face even cancer with patience and endurance. When we surrender our natural, carnal inclination to complain and instead let God clothe us with His peace, He transforms our perspective. Suddenly, the storm is no longer the loudest voice in the room. He is.

As we lean into His promises, we find the strength to care for our husbands with renewed compassion and love. We find the patience to endure another day. And we find the hope of eternal life shining like a steady light, even when everything around us seems dark. That hope reminds us that cancer does not have the final word. God does.

Say this out loud: **I am encouraged by God.**

Now declare this: **I declare that the Scriptures give me endurance, encouragement, and hope as I walk through trials.**

This verse reminds us that the Scriptures were written not only for past generations but also for us today. In them, we find the encouragement and strength we need to endure life's trials. God's Word anchors us in hope, teaching us patience in seasons of waiting and reassuring us that His promises are trustworthy. For caregivers and those navigating grief, the Scriptures serve as both a guide and a lifeline, reminding us that our story is in God's hands.

Prayer of Reflection

Lord, I thank You for the gift of Your Word. In my moments of weakness and discouragement, remind me to turn to the Scriptures, where I find strength to endure and encouragement to press on. When I grow weary in caregiving or heavy with grief, let Your promises be the anchor that steadies my heart. Fill me with hope that is rooted not in circumstances but in Your unchanging truth. Teach me to wait patiently, trust deeply, and cling to the assurance that every word You have spoken is faithful. Amen.

May the God of your hope so fill you with all joy and peace in believing [through the experience of your faith] that by the power of the Holy Spirit you may abound and be overflowing (bubbling over) with hope. Romans 15:13

Doug and I were enjoying our weekly steak dinner from a local restaurant. A small but sacred ritual that had become our way of marking each week of chemotherapy treatment. Someone had given us a gift certificate early in his diagnosis, and from that moment on, we decided it would become a weekly act of celebration—a reminder that even in the midst of battle, we could still find joy.

Every Tuesday, after treatment, I would place our order online and pick it up on our way home. Doug's immune system was too fragile for public places, so we made our kitchen table our favorite restaurant. I would light a candle, set out our plates, and we would bow our heads in prayer, thanking God for His provision for another day, another meal, another moment of peace.

By this point in our journey, Doug was nearing the end of a long round of chemotherapy. Remarkably, he would walk three to five miles a day with our loyal dog, Spot, even on chemotherapy days. His resilience amazed me. Alongside his medical treatment, he was faithfully taking the Chinese herbal supplements we had chosen as an alternative therapy. The supplements were expensive and while he never knew the true financial strain, I quietly carried that burden, juggling bills and shifting funds with faith that God would make a way.

I was still working then, taking time off on Tuesdays to be by his side for treatments. My employer graciously allowed me the flexibility I needed, a blessing I didn't take for granted. Those small mercies

— time off, financial provision, strength for each new day — were God's fingerprints of grace on our journey.

That evening, Doug took a bite of his steak, smiled, and said, "I feel great after this treatment." His optimism was contagious. For the first time in a long while, we allowed ourselves to dream again — to imagine a future where cancer didn't dictate the rhythm of our lives. We talked about traveling, visiting family, and even taking Spot on longer walks through the mountains once he felt stronger.

In that quiet evening, sitting across from him at the table, I felt something rise in my spirit — *hope*. Not the kind that ignores reality, but the kind that comes from knowing God's hand was still on our lives. The same God who had carried us through the darkest days was still writing our story.

That night, the verse from Romans 15:13 came alive for me: *"May the God of hope fill you with all joy and peace as you trust in Him."* Hope wasn't about the outcome; it was about the overflow. It was about finding joy in the present moment, peace in the process, and trust in the God who never left our side.

For a brief, beautiful time, hope filled our home again — and that hope, born of the Holy Spirit, carried us through every step that followed.

Say this out loud: **I am living in the overflow of hope.**

Now declare this: **I declare that the God of hope fills me with all joy and peace as I trust in Him, so that I overflow with hope by the power of the Holy Spirit.**

Paul, the author of Romans, reminds us that God Himself is the source of true hope. As we place our trust in Him, He fills us with joy and peace—not as fleeting emotions, but as steady gifts that sustain us through trials. This hope is not dependent on circumstances but flows from the power of the Holy Spirit within us. For caregivers and those grieving, this verse offers assurance that even in seasons of exhaustion or sorrow, God's Spirit enables us to overflow with hope that cannot be shaken.

Prayer of Reflection

God of hope, I come to You weary and often overwhelmed, yet trusting that You alone are the source of joy and peace. Fill me with Your Spirit when my own strength runs dry. Let Your joy steady me when sadness rises, and let Your peace guard my heart when worry tries to take over.

Lord, I ask that You cause my hope to overflow, not just enough for me, but enough to spill into the lives of those I love and care for. May my words, my actions, and even my quiet prayers be marked by the hope of Christ that shines brighter than sorrow. Keep reminding me that my circumstances do not define me; Your Spirit within me does. Amen.

The Lord is my portion or share, says my living being (my inner self); therefore will I hope in Him and wait expectantly for Him. The Lord is good to those who wait hopefully and expectantly for Him, to those who seek Him [inquire of and for Him and require Him by right of necessity and on the authority of God's word]. It is good that one should hope in and wait quietly for the salvation (the safety and ease) of the Lord. Lamentations 3:24-26

I recently had a friend share her health struggles with me — yet another autoimmune disease added to the long list of ailments she was battling. Without hesitation, I looked her in the eye and said, "That is *not* your portion."

In that moment, my words took me back to the day Doug and I received the news that would change our lives forever. The day we learned that he indeed had stage 4 lung cancer. Until then, we had held onto a flicker of hope that the tumor found in his lung might be contained. Though the tumor seemed large to us, we believed it could be easily treated. *"Easy peasy,"* Doug had said with his usual optimism. *"I'm going to kick this to the curb."*

But that hope was shattered when we were told that the cancer had spread to his brain. Looking back, it all made sense — the headaches behind his eyes that no medication or eye surgery could relieve, the hearing loss that even his hearing aids couldn't fix, the fatigue that had begun to shadow his once boundless energy. The brain lesion was in his left occipital lobe, the source of so many unexplained symptoms.

And in that moment, I wanted to scream, *"This is not his portion!"* Because I knew what God's Word says: that His desire for us is health, peace, and prosperity of soul. Good health is our portion in the Lord. Abundant life is our portion. Healing is our portion. And yet, the reality before us told a different story.

That was the beginning of our struggle to reconcile what we saw with what we believed. We found ourselves living in the tension between heaven's promises and earth's pain. It forced us to lean hard into God's Word — to cling to His character even when the outcome didn't make sense.

We had to learn, as the prophet Jeremiah wrote in *Lamentations 3:24-26,* to wait quietly and hope for the Lord's salvation. Waiting and hoping are not passive acts. They are spiritual disciplines — deliberate choices to anchor our hearts in God's goodness while walking through the valley of uncertainty.

Waiting doesn't mean inactivity; it means resting in the assurance that God is working even when we can't see it. Hoping doesn't mean denying reality; it means declaring that reality isn't the end of the story.

Doug and I waited — sometimes in tears, sometimes in worship, sometimes in the quiet exhaustion that caregiving brings. But even in those moments of anguish, God's faithfulness became our lifeline. The truth we held onto was this: though our bodies may fail, our hope in Him never will.

His mercies were new every morning, fresh hope for every step of the journey. And when the days were dark and the diagnosis overwhelming, we could still say, "The Lord is my portion; therefore, I will hope in Him."

Say this out loud: **The Lord is my portion, and I hope only in Him.**

Now declare this: **I declare that the Lord is my portion, and I will place my hope in Him, waiting quietly and trusting in His goodness and salvation.**

These verses remind us that even in seasons of grief and loss, we can anchor our hearts in the unchanging truth that the Lord Himself is our portion. When everything else feels uncertain or stripped away, God's presence and promises remain. We are invited to wait quietly, not in despair, but in trust knowing that His goodness never fails and His salvation always comes. For caregivers and those grieving, this passage offers comfort that our hope is secure when it rests in Him alone.

Prayer of Reflection

Lord, when everything around me feels uncertain, I take comfort in knowing that You are my portion and my hope. Thank You that Your presence is enough to sustain me when my strength fails and when my heart feels empty.

Teach me to wait quietly before You, not with despair, but with trust that Your goodness is always at work, even when I cannot see it. Remind me that Your mercies are new every morning and that Your salvation never fails. As I walk through caregiving and grief, let my soul find rest in You alone, and may my hope in You grow stronger each day. Amen.

Confessions of Faith

For we hold that a man is justified and made upright
by faith independent of and distinctly apart from good
deeds (works of the Law). [The observance of the Law has
nothing to do with justification.] Romans 3:28

When our husbands are sick, our faith as wives and caregivers is certainly tested. It is in those moments that we are reminded that our faith is not in ourselves, not in medicine, not even in our caregiving abilities; it is in Christ alone. Real faith produces good works, but our works do not save us. Our mindset must remain fixed on Christ, not on the good works we perform. For it is not our striving or our fleshly effort that makes us right before God, but the works we do in obedience to our Father in Heaven.

God is so good to us. Scripture tells us plainly that all *have sinned and fall short of the glory of God.* None of us can earn His favor by being "good enough," not even by being the most faithful wife or tireless caregiver. Our righteousness comes only through faith in Jesus Christ. His grace, freely given, imparts to us eternal life and releases us from the guilt and condemnation of sin. Grace is our undeserved gift, bought and secured through the finished work of Jesus Christ on the Cross.

In the messy middle of a cancer journey, however, it is easy to lose sight of this truth. Our eyes can shift from the One who is above to the circumstances that are right in front of us. We may begin measuring ourselves by what we do or how well we serve, forgetting that God's love for us does not rise and fall with our performance. It is a delicate balance to keep our hearts and minds turned toward God while also pouring our energy into caring for our husbands day after day.

Yet, even in the midst of our caregiving, God remains at work. He is shaping us, refining us, and molding us into the women He has called us to be. His Word tells us that He has predestined us with a future and a purpose, one that cancer cannot erase and suffering cannot undo. This season is not wasted. It is part of the God-ordained destiny He has written for our lives.

Satan would love for us to believe otherwise. He whispers lies that we are incompetent as caregivers, worthless as wives, and hopeless as women. But those lies crumble before the truth of God's Word: *by faith, we are made righteous.* Our confidence does not come from ourselves, but from the God who dwells within us. Through the death and resurrection of Jesus Christ, the seed of righteousness has been sown in us, and we are clothed in His victory.

God is reminding us daily that we stand accepted and justified in His presence. Our husbands' illnesses are not our identity, nor is it our portion to carry as our own. Our portion is Christ Himself and every promise He has given us. Because of Him, we can declare with confidence that we will not only get through this trial, we will overcome it. Every obstacle and every setback is met with the assurance of His victory.

We are justified by faith in Christ alone. And because of that justification, we can endure suffering without despair, love without measure, and trust without fear. In Christ, we are not victims of our circumstances; we are victors through faith.

Say this out loud: **God prospers me in every way. He keeps my body and soul well.**

Now declare this: **I declare that it is God's will for me to prosper and be in good health, even as my soul prospers in Him.**

Paul reminds us that we are made right with God through faith, apart from the works of the law. No amount of striving, effort, or good deeds can earn us righteousness—it is a gift of grace received through trusting in Christ. For caregivers and those in seasons of trial, this truth is freeing: our value is not in how perfectly we serve, but in the finished work of Jesus. Faith in Him alone secures our right standing with God and gives us peace in the midst of life's burdens.

Prayer of Reflection

Lord, thank You that my righteousness does not come from what I do but from who I am in Christ. In the exhausting work of caregiving, I often feel like I fall short—tired, overwhelmed, and unsure if I am enough. But You remind me that my worth is not measured by my performance, and my standing with You is not determined by my works.

Thank You, Jesus, for the Cross, where You bore my sin, my shame, and my striving, and gave me the gift of Your righteousness. Teach me to rest in Your grace when my flesh wants to prove itself. Remind me that my portion is not sickness, despair, or hopelessness—my portion is Christ and His victory.

When the enemy whispers that I am incompetent or unworthy, silence his lies with the truth of Your Word. Shape me, mold me, and help me to walk boldly in the destiny You have ordained for me. Let my life reflect the confidence that comes from faith in You alone, and may Your strength be seen in my weakness. Amen.

Truly I tell you, whoever says to this mountain, be lifted up and thrown into the sea! and does not doubt at all in his heart but believes that what he says will take place, it will be done for him. For this reason I am telling you, whatever you ask for in prayer, believe (trust and be confident) that it is granted to you, and you will [get it]. And whenever you stand praying, if you have anything against anyone, forgive him and let it drop (leave it, let it go), in order that your Father Who is in heaven may also forgive you your [own] failings and shortcomings and let them drop. Mark 11:23-25

This passage in the Bible is written in red letters, Jesus' own words. He is the Word, and when He speaks about faith, He is not merely giving a suggestion; He is revealing the heart of God. In these verses, Jesus is literally talking about having the faith of God.

But what is faith? From the very beginning, humanity was created by the faith of God. He spoke, and the world came into being. Yet, at the fall in the Garden of Eden, doubt entered the equation, and humankind's ability to walk fully in faith was fractured. The good news is that faith is restored in us through our new birth in Christ. Just as a muscle grows to fullness and strength when exercised and maintained, faith also grows to fullness and strength when exercised and maintained.

Jesus makes it clear: faith without doubting is the condition we must meet to experience the full power of God's promises. His words assure us that this promise is for everyone who believes in Him. When we pray with faith, without wavering in our hearts, our prayers are heard—and they are answered. The answers may not always come in the way we expect, but God always keeps His Word. His promise is unshakable: when we pray according to His will, we can trust Him to respond.

Helpful ways to practice prayerful intimacy with God:
- Have the faith of God. (Romans 4:17; Hebrews 11:3; Galatians 5:22-23)

- Pray and speak clearly what you are asking for. (Mark 11:23-24; Matthew 17:20; Matthew 21:21-22; John 15:7)

- Do not limit God's will or power—have unlimited faith. (Mark 11:23-24; Matthew 17:20; Matthew 21:21-22; Mark 9:23; John 15: 7, 16)

- Refuse to doubt in your heart. (Mark 11:23; Matthew 17:20; James 1:5-8)

- Believe that whatever you ask will be given. (Mark 11:23-24; Matthew 7:7-11; Matthew 17:20; Matthew 21:21- 22; Hebrews 11:6)

- Believe that what you have asked for is already given. (Mark 11:24; Matthew 17:20; 1 John 5:14-15)

- Use the authority God has given you to declare His promises. (Mark 11:23-24; Matthew 17:20; Mark 9:23)

- Believe that what you want aligns with God's will. (Mark 11:24; John 15:7; Matthew 17:20; Matthew 21:21-22; Hebrews 11:6; James 1:5-8)

- If it is promised in God's Word, do not weaken it by saying,

"If it be Thy will." (Mark 11:23; Psalm 84:11

- 2 Corinthians 1:20; 2 Peter 1:3-4)

- Maintain a pure heart before God and in your relationships with others. (Mark 11:25; John 15:7; 1 John 3:22-23)

Jesus also reminds us that the words we speak reflect the condition of our hearts. As caregivers, this becomes especially important. It is easy to be swayed by the words of doctors, medical professionals, friends, or even family members. Those words, spoken with or without intent, can shape our emotions, build fear, or plant seeds of doubt in our spirits. And when we repeat them, we risk speaking death over ourselves instead of life.

Only the Word of God offers the encouragement, correction, and truth we need. His Word is living and active, perfectly timed for every step of our journey. As caregivers, we must train ourselves to feast on Scripture, rather than succumbing to the negativity that surrounds us. Only God's Word has the power to correct our hearts, renew our minds, and sustain us in righteousness.

We must guard our mouths carefully, because our thoughts eventually find their way into our speech. This is why Paul urges us to be transformed by the renewing of our minds daily so that our thoughts, and therefore our words, reflect the truth of God rather than the fears of our flesh. Faith *comes by hearing, and hearing by the Word of God (Romans 10:17)*. The more we saturate ourselves in His promises, the stronger our faith grows.

God invites us to live from *faith to faith,* to keep moving forward, not in our own strength, but in the assurance of His glory, His righteousness, His presence, and His power. Faith is not complicated; it is simply believing that God is who He says He is and that His promises are true. As caregivers, when we live and speak from that place of faith, we invite His peace, His strength, and His hope to carry us through.

Say this out loud: **I believe what God says is true.**

Now declare this: **I declare that by faith in God, every mountain before me will move in His power and timing, and I will trust Him as my strength in the caregiving journey.**

Jesus teaches that even the greatest mountains can be moved through faith-filled prayer. For caregivers, the weight of cancer can feel like an immovable mountain too heavy to bear, too overwhelming to climb. Yet Jesus reminds us that with faith, we can speak to those mountains, trusting God to move them in His power and timing. This does not always mean the mountain disappears instantly, but it does mean we are not left to climb it alone. God reveals His strength not to the proud or self-sufficient, but to the humble who depend on Him. As we walk through caregiving with faith, we discover that He is both the mover of mountains and the sustainer of our hearts.

Prayer of Reflection

Lord Jesus, You taught us that mountains can be moved when we pray with faith and do not doubt. In this season of caregiving, the mountain before me often feels immovable—the weight of cancer, the exhaustion of daily care, and the fear of what lies ahead. Yet You remind me that nothing is impossible with God.

Help me to speak words of faith instead of fear, to lift up prayers with confidence that You hear me, and to trust that You are working even when I cannot see. Teach me to release my doubts and rest in the truth that You are my Healer, my Sustainer, and my Deliverer.

Thank You, Father, that You reveal Your strength not to the wise and strong of the world but to the humble who depend on You. I choose to depend on You now. Strengthen my faith, steady my heart, and help me to care for my loved one with courage and hope that comes from Your Spirit. Amen.

So also faith, if it does not have works (deeds and actions of obedience to back it up), by itself is destitute of power (inoperative, dead). James 2:17

What James is teaching us is clear: it does no good to simply say we have faith if our actions do not reflect that faith. Words without deeds are empty. One commentary illustrates it this way: there can be no fire without fuel, and no fuel without fire. To claim one without the other is contrary to the very laws that govern them. In the same way, true faith will always produce works, and true works will always flow from faith.

Scripture provides a perfect demonstration in the story of Abraham. When God asked him to offer Isaac as a sacrifice, it was not a blind ritual; it was an act of faith. Abraham trusted God so completely that he obeyed, believing that God's promise would prevail no matter the outcome. His faith was proven genuine by his obedience, and his obedience was sustained by his faith. The two cannot be separated.

As caregivers, this principle becomes deeply personal. Faith is not just an abstract belief we hold in our minds; it is something we live out every day in how we love, serve, and endure. It is faith that motivates us to get out of bed when exhaustion weighs heavily on us. It is faith that strengthens our hands to prepare meals, manage medications, or sit through long nights beside our husbands. It is faith that keeps us praying for healing, even when the reports sound grim. And it is faith that gives us the courage to speak life when everything around us feels marked by death.

Without faith, our caregiving quickly becomes nothing more than duty, drained of hope. But with faith, our caregiving becomes a testimony, a visible sign that God is sustaining us, guiding us, and working through us. Just as Abraham's faith was counted as righteousness, so our quiet acts of service, done in faith, become an offering to God.

Faith and works are inseparable. Faith without works is dead, and works without faith are empty. But when the two are joined together, they create a fire that not only sustains us but also becomes a light to others who are walking through their own valleys.

Say this out loud: **I believe that faith without works is dead.**

Now declare this: **I declare that my faith is alive and proven genuine through the works of love and obedience God enables me to do.**

James reminds us that faith without works is dead. True faith is not just something we claim to have; it must be evident in how we live our lives. For caregivers, this truth holds particular significance. Our daily acts of love, service, and perseverance are not meaningless duties; they are living expressions of faith in God. When our actions align with our trust in Him, our caregiving becomes both a testimony of His strength and an offering of worship. Faith and works cannot be separated—together, they reveal the life of Christ within us.

Prayer of Reflection

Lord, thank You for teaching me that true faith is always revealed in action. Forgive me for the times I have claimed faith with my words but struggled to live it out with my deeds. In this season of caregiving, I confess that it is not easy to keep going when I am weary and discouraged, yet I know You are the One who gives me strength.

Help me, Lord, to let my actions testify to the faith I hold in You. May every meal I prepare, every doctor's appointment I sit through, and every prayer I whisper over my husband be an offering of obedience and love. Strengthen my faith so that it fuels my works, and let my works, in turn, prove the reality of my faith.

Just as Abraham trusted You and acted in obedience, help me to walk in that same kind of trust, believing that You are faithful to Your promises. Let my caregiving be more than duty, let it be a living testimony of Your sustaining grace and a light to others who are watching. Amen.

for we walk by faith, not by sight [living our lives in
a manner consistent with our confident belief in God's
promises] 2 Corinthians 5:7

The greatest lesson I learned as a cancer-fighting wife is that man can only see what is in front of him — what can be touched, tested, or measured. But as followers of Christ, we are called to live by faith, not by sight. Faith allows us to see beyond what is visible and into what is eternal.

So many of us live our daily lives unaware of how close heaven truly is. The veil between the seen and unseen isn't far away — it's right here, a breath, a heartbeat away. It is thin, sacred, and ever-present. And when I walked this cancer journey with Doug, I began to sense how near eternity really is.

Doug and I learned to live in such a way that our faith became our testimony. We chose to believe God's promises for our lives and for the generations that would follow us — our children and our children's children. We lived with a heavenly perspective, not because it was easy, but because it was necessary to survive the storm.

Along the way, there were those who didn't understand. Some of our extended family questioned our choices, doubted our faith, or argued that we should "trust the science" above all else. Their words could be sharp, especially near the end, when Doug's condition worsened. Even in his final days, as he drifted between this world and the next, I heard whispers of accusation — that perhaps the medication was too strong, that faith had gone too far. But I knew better. I had seen the peace that settled over him, the light that seemed to fill his room, the reverence that silenced every fear.

In my caregiving, I had also learned something sobering about modern medicine. At the end of life, medication is often given not only to ease the patient's pain but also to calm the distress of those keeping vigil. The living are comforted by what numbs the dying — but for those who belong to Jesus, there is no fear in that final passage. The dying see what the living cannot. The veil parts, and heaven draws near.

I know my husband saw beyond that veil. About five days before he passed, he looked toward me and asked softly, *"Who is behind you?"* I turned and said, "The angels are here." He nodded and said, "I see them."

In the days that followed, I often caught him raising his hands — not out of confusion or delirium, but in worship. He was praising His Lord and Savior, even from his deathbed. I would stand in the doorway, quietly watching, tears in my eyes, realizing I was witnessing something holy — a man walking by faith right into the arms of eternity.

We will all one day lay down our mortal bodies. This truth once terrified me, but now it comforts me. For those who believe, death is not the end — it is the continuation of the story. To be absent from the body is to be present with the Lord. That is the faith we live by.

Yes, I miss Doug deeply. I ache for his voice, his laughter, his presence beside me. And though Scripture tells us there is no marriage in heaven, I take joy in knowing that he and I will meet again — redeemed, whole, and glorified. I imagine that in Heaven, I'll visit his house and we'll walk together once more, as friends and fellow worshipers, gathered in the eternal fellowship of our Lord Jesus Christ.

And until that day comes, I will keep walking by faith, not by sight — because faith has shown me that love never dies; it simply crosses the veil.

Say this out loud: **I walk by faith and am confident in God's promises.**

Now declare this: **I declare that I walk by faith and not by sight, trusting God's promises even when I cannot see the way forward.**

The Christian life is not guided by what we see or understand in the natural world, but by trusting in God's promises. Sight is limited to circumstances, but faith looks beyond to the eternal. For caregivers and those walking through grief, this means we don't place our confidence in medical reports, emotions, or visible outcomes. Instead, we live anchored in God's Word and His faithfulness, knowing that even when the path is unclear, He is leading us step by step.

Prayer of Reflection

Lord, thank You for reminding me that my life is not guided by what I see, but by faith in You. When the reports are grim, when the path feels unclear, and when my heart is heavy with grief, teach me to trust Your promises more than my circumstances.

Help me to walk step by step in faith, believing that You are with me even when I cannot see the way ahead. Strengthen me to lean on Your Word as my guide and let my hope rest not in what is visible but in Your eternal faithfulness. Remind me that every step of faith brings me closer to You. Amen.

But without faith it is impossible to [walk with God and] please Him, for whoever comes [near] to God must [necessarily] believe that God exists and that He rewards those who [earnestly and diligently] seek Him. Hebrews 11:6

Sitting in the emergency room beside Doug, I felt the edges of my faith fraying. The sterile white lights above hummed softly as nurses hurried in and out, starting an IV to hydrate him and preparing him for a CT scan. Machines beeped rhythmically, echoing the uneven rhythm of my own heartbeat.

Doug couldn't answer the simplest questions the nurse asked — his name, the date, or the name of the president. Each time he looked at me for help, my heart ached. I wanted to speak for him, to fill in the blanks, to somehow make this all easier for him. But I couldn't. The nurses needed to know what he could remember. They needed to see the decline that I had been quietly fearing for hours.

"I think he's dehydrated," I explained, my voice trembling as I searched for hope in the words. "He's been struggling to drink enough water, and the oncology center has been giving him fluids." But even as I spoke, I knew deep down that this was more than dehydration. Something deeper, more serious, was happening — and I could feel the weight of it pressing against my chest.

In that moment, fear crept in and tried to replace faith. My prayers felt small and fragile. My faith, which had once felt steady and sure, seemed to falter under the sterile glow of that emergency room light. I knew God was real. I had seen His faithfulness over and over again in our journey. But right then, I couldn't feel Him.

Doug, ever the fighter, brushed off the nurses' concern. He didn't want to be there. He wanted to go home — to his chair, to his comfort, to his familiar. He didn't understand the urgency. And while he seemed at peace in his confusion, I was unraveling in mine. I wanted to believe that God was near, that He was still holding us, but everything in me was trembling with uncertainty.

"Without faith, it is impossible to please Him." Those words from Hebrews 11:6 echoed in my mind, not as condemnation, but as a gentle reminder to trust in God. Faith isn't about feeling strong; it's about choosing to believe when everything feels weak. It's about clinging to the truth that God exists — not just in the church sanctuary, but in hospital rooms, in diagnoses, and in moments of complete helplessness.

That day, my faith didn't look bold or triumphant. It looked like whispered prayers under my breath. It looked like holding Doug's hand and refusing to let go. It looked like sitting in silence and still daring to hope that God was near, even when I couldn't sense His presence.

Faith isn't the absence of fear — it's the act of turning toward God in the middle of it. And in that small, trembling faith, I found Him again — not in the miracle I hoped for, but in the strength to keep believing when everything else was falling apart.

Say this out loud: **I believe that God exists, and I walk with Him.**

Now declare this: **I declare that I believe God exists, I seek Him diligently, and I trust that He rewards my faith as I walk with Him.**

Hebrews 11:6 reminds us that faith is essential to our relationship with God. Without faith, we cannot please Him, for faith is the foundation of trust and intimacy with Him. To draw near, we must believe that He is real, present, and active in our lives, and that He rewards those who earnestly seek Him. For caregivers and those navigating grief, this verse serves as a reminder that even when circumstances seem overwhelming, God honors sincere faith. He promises to meet us with His presence, His strength, and His reward when we seek Him with our whole hearts.

Prayer of Reflection

Lord, Your Word tells me that without faith it is impossible to please You. Some days, my faith feels small and fragile, especially when the weight of caregiving and grief presses in. Yet I choose to believe that You are real, that You are with me, and that You reward those who earnestly seek You.

Teach me to walk with You in faith even when I cannot see the outcome. Strengthen my trust that You hear my prayers, hold my tears, and honor the faith I bring before You. Help me to seek You diligently, not only in moments of crisis but in the quiet, ordinary moments of each day. May my life, even in suffering, be a testimony of faith that pleases You. Amen.

Confessions of Depression

It is the Lord Who goes before you; He will [march] with you; He will not fail you or let you go or forsake you; [let there be no cowardice or flinching, but] fear not, neither become broken [in spirit—depressed, dismayed, and unnerved with alarm]. Deuteronomy 31:8

Depression, desperation, and dismay are all valid feelings when a husband is facing a cancer diagnosis. There is no sugar-coating the reality: at some point on this journey, we will face depression. The Bible does not deny our emotions but calls us to anchor them in God's truth.

When Moses gave his final instructions to Israel and to Joshua, he gave them both the same commands—and with those commands, the same promises. God, in His goodness, promised that He would not fail them, nor would He forsake them. That same promise is ours today. But how do we hold onto that assurance without losing our faith and our way in the middle of the cancer journey?

We hold fast by putting our faith into action and refusing to become broken in spirit. In the messy middle, it is easy to throw in the towel, give up, or listen to the whispers of the enemy. Over and over, he murmurs that we have lost—that cancer has already won and that hope is gone. The insidious softness of his lies can become deafening, driving a weary heart toward despair.

But dismay comes when we march forward alone, independent of the covering of the Lord. God never intended us to carry the battle by ourselves. He goes before us. He marches with us. He leads us. He is not a God of failure—He is the God of victory.

When we look closely at God's instruction in Deuteronomy, the words that stand out are these: *"let there be no cowardice or flinching."* To flinch is to shrink back in the face of suffering, to withdraw when pain or danger is present, or to fail to keep moving forward. As caregivers and wives of men fighting cancer, we know the cost of this journey. We have suffered in body and spirit as we walk with our loved ones through their battle. Yet what captures my heart in this verse is the warning against *"failing to proceed."* Proceed means to move forward, to continue toward something greater. As wives and caregivers, we cannot flinch. We must not stop. Even when our hearts ache, even when the danger of losing ourselves feels real, we are called to move forward with courage and hope, trusting the God who leads us.

Moses gave Israel and Joshua three simple, yet profound, instructions from God:

Be strong.

Be of good courage.

Be not afraid.

I have heard many people tell me, "You're so strong. You're so courageous. You're unafraid." But the truth is, most of the time I feel none of those things. Strength and courage do not come naturally in the middle of cancer's storm. They only come when I dive into God's Word and remind myself that He is the One who goes before me. It is His presence, not my own willpower, that allows me to face each day with courage instead of fear.

This is why we must examine our hearts. Are we walking this journey in our own strength, relying only on ourselves? Or are we proceeding—moving forward—in the strength and hope that God is in control, that He is leading us, and that His victory is assured?

Isaiah 54:4 reminds us: *"Fear not, for you shall not be ashamed; neither be confounded and depressed, for you shall not be put to shame. For you shall forget the shame of your youth, and you shall not [seriously] remember the reproach of your widowhood any more."*

When depression grips us in the face of cancer, it is easy to become fearful, distrustful, and unbelieving. Yet God instructs us to "fear not"—to trust Him even in the hardest places. Sometimes we even feel shame about our depression, as though we are failing in our faith because of it. But here is the good news: depression and shame are normal human emotions when faced with something as devastating as a life-threatening illness. The issue is not whether we feel these things—it is what we do with them that matters.

For those who hear God's voice, we know that He listens to our cries and petitions. He is not punishing us or our husbands through cancer. That is not who He is. God is a kind, compassionate Father who calls us to follow His leading. He cares deeply for us. He loves us—even in the dark valley of sickness and loss.

So we can rest in His embrace. We must learn to stop thinking at a low, earthly level, confined to what we see and understand. Instead, we must lift our eyes to the spiritual truth of who we are in Him. We are spirits with bodies and souls, and we must learn to see beyond the physical to what is ours in Christ.

Through Jesus, we can disrobe ourselves of shame and depression and put on the robe that was always meant for us—the robe of righteousness and wholeness. On the Cross, Jesus bore our sicknesses, our sorrows, and our sins. He carried the full weight of our brokenness so that we could be made new. Because of Him, we are not defined by cancer, depression, or despair. We are defined by His victory.

Say this out loud: **The Lord will not fail me.**

Now declare this: **I declare that the Lord goes before me, stays with me, and will never leave or forsake me, so I will not fear or be discouraged.**

This verse is a powerful reminder that we never walk into the unknown alone. Just as God promised Joshua and Israel that He would go before them into the battles ahead, He promises us the same today. For caregivers and those facing the trial of cancer, this truth offers deep comfort: God Himself goes ahead to prepare the way, He walks beside us to give strength, and He never abandons us in our weakness. Because His presence is constant and His promises are sure, we can face tomorrow with confidence and hope.

Prayer of Reflection

Lord, thank You for the promise that You go before me, that You stay with me, and that You will never leave or forsake me. In the hard places of caregiving, when fear rises and discouragement feels overwhelming, remind me that I am never walking this path alone.

Teach me to lean on Your presence when my strength fails and to trust that You are already preparing the way ahead for me. Replace my fear with courage, my discouragement with hope, and my weariness with Your strength. Help me to rest in the truth that because You are with me, I can keep moving forward in faith. Amen.

Therefore humble yourselves [demote, lower yourselves in your own estimation] under the mighty hand of God, that in due time He may exalt you, Casting the whole of your care [all your anxieties, all your worries, all your concerns, once and for all] on Him, for He cares for you affectionately and cares about you watchfully. 1 Peter 5:6-7

God's Word teaches us to cast all our burdens on Him, for He alone is able to carry them (1 Peter 5:7). What a relief it is to know that we don't have to hold it all together in our own strength. God's shoulders are big enough to bear every fear, every worry, and every heartbreak we face. He knows exactly what each of us is going through on this journey of walking with a loved one through cancer.

Even in seasons of depression—when the weight of caregiving feels crushing and hope seems far away—our lives still speak a testimony to others. Everything we say, everything we do, and even how we respond in our pain reveals something about God to others. That is both humbling and encouraging, because it reminds us that we are never walking through our trials unnoticed.

Scripture tells us that God *"cares about us watchfully."* This means He is not distant or indifferent but deeply engaged in our lives. He is vigilant, always watching over us with careful attention. He sees the things no one else sees. He heeds our needs before we can even voice them. He tenderly guards and comforts His children, even when we feel too weary to notice His presence.

No matter how low our thoughts may sink, no matter how lonely or misunderstood we feel in our suffering, God understands. He knows the pain behind every sigh, the meaning behind every tear, and the burden behind every sleepless night. While others may not fully grasp what we carry, He does. And more than that—He loves us with an affection that never wavers and a devotion that never ends.

Our promise in this Scripture is not only that God carries our burdens but also that He will exalt us in due time. To exalt means to raise us up—to lift us out of despair and into His joy, His confidence, and ultimately His victory. It doesn't mean the journey will be easy or the road free of pain, but it does mean that He will not leave us where we are. He will raise us, renew us, and restore us in His perfect timing.

So we cast our burdens on Him not just once, but over and over again, as often as the weight threatens to overwhelm us. In return, we receive His peace, His strength, and the promise that one day He will lift us high above the shadows of our suffering.

Say this out loud: **I am cared for by my God.**

Now declare this: **I declare that I humble myself under God's mighty hand, casting all my cares on Him, for He cares for me affectionately.**

Peter reminds us that humility and trust are key to walking with God in difficult seasons. To humble ourselves under His mighty hand is to acknowledge that we cannot carry life's burdens on our own. Instead, we release our anxieties, fears, and struggles to Him, knowing that He cares for us deeply and watches over us with love. For caregivers and those grieving, this is a lifeline: we don't have to carry the crushing weight of illness or loss alone. God invites us to lay it all at His feet, trusting that He will lift us up in His timing and sustain us with His care.

Prayer of Reflection

Lord, I humble myself under Your mighty hand, confessing that I cannot carry the weight of this journey on my own. The fears, the worries, and the exhaustion feel too heavy, but I thank You that I don't have to bear them alone.

Today I choose to cast every care—every doctor's report, every sleepless night, every wave of grief—into Your hands. Thank You that You care for me not distantly but personally, with love and watchfulness. Remind me each day that You see me, You know my burdens, and You are faithful to sustain me. Lift me up in Your timing, and help me to rest in the safety of Your care. Amen.

Arise [from the depression and prostration in which cir-
cumstances have kept you—rise to a new life]! Shine (be
radiant with the glory of the Lord), for your light has come,
and the glory of the Lord has risen upon you! Isaiah 60:1

God promises us new life and healing for our brokenness. As caregivers, there is no denying the reality: walking alongside a loved one diagnosed with terminal cancer wounds the soul and breaks the spirit. The constant strain, the relentless uncertainty, and the weight of grief carve deep, sorrowful places within us. And it is just like the enemy of our souls—the devil—to use these circumstances to keep us trapped in depression, oppression, and the suffocating darkness of despair.

But God commands us in Isaiah to rise up: *"Arise, shine, for your light has come, and the glory of the Lord rises upon you"* (Isaiah 60:1). This is not a gentle suggestion; it is a command to lift our heads, stand in faith, and receive His promise. He assures us that His glory will fill our spirits and transform our countenance, making us radiant with His love. His glory has already risen upon us! Through His presence, He brings full restoration into our lives and covers us, and our loved ones, under His healing wings. Even in the hardest circumstances, He offers wholeness and hope.

But what is God's glory? It is the manifestation of all that He is—the fullness of His perfection, majesty, and power. Jesus Himself declared in the book of John that He was the earthly manifestation of His Heavenly Father's glory. God communicates His glory through creation, through His Word, and through His image-bearers—you and me. As His children, we carry His image and are united to Him through Christ. When we glorify Him as our Father in Heaven, He, in turn, bestows His glory upon us, covering us with His love, His light, and His power.

Even in seasons of suffering, God desires to bless us. When we received Christ as Savior, it marked not the end but the beginning of our relationship with Him. That relationship is intimate and personal. He knows every detail of what we are going through, and He cares deeply. His glory is not far off; it meets us where we are, even in the hospital room, even in the quiet tears at night, even in the exhaustion of daily caregiving.

So, arise! Believe that God will meet you in your brokenness. Believe that His presence will fill the dark places with light. Believe that His glory is already upon you and that He will carry you into restoration, healing, and wholeness—both now and in eternity.

Say this out loud: **I am filled with the Glory of God.**

Now declare this: **I declare that I will arise and shine, for the light of God's glory has risen upon me and fills me with His radiance.**

Isaiah 60:1 is a call to action. God commands His people to rise up and reflect His glory. In seasons of grief, weariness, or caregiving, it can feel easier to succumb to the weight of sorrow. Yet this verse reminds us that God's light has already come, and His glory is upon us. We are not asked to shine in our own strength but to reflect the radiance of His presence. This is both a promise and an invitation: no matter how dark the night, God's glory covers His children and empowers us to walk forward in hope.

Prayer of Reflection

Lord, You call me to arise and shine because Your light has come and Your glory rests upon me. Some days, the weight of grief and caregiving feels too heavy to rise, and my spirit feels too dim to shine. Yet I thank You that Your command is not a burden but an invitation to live in the strength of Your presence.

Lift me from the heaviness of despair and clothe me with the radiance of Your glory. Teach me to reflect Your light even in the darkest valleys, so that others may see Your hope shining through me. Remind me that I do not carry this calling alone—Your Spirit within me empowers me to stand, to shine, and to trust that Your glory is greater than my pain. Amen.

But God, Who comforts and encourages and refreshes and cheers the depressed and the sinking, comforted and encouraged and refreshed and cheered us by the arrival of Titus. 2 Corinthians 7:6

We suffer from depression when we experience grief and sorrow from many different circumstances. In this particular journey, the sorrow comes from watching a loved one face cancer, and often, the prospect of death. The fear that surrounds cancer is overwhelming, both for patients and caregivers. History has shown us generations of families and communities touched by the devastation of this disease. Billions, even trillions, of dollars have been poured into research and treatment by governments and private companies, yet cancer remains a persistent and destructive force. For many, it has become not only a medical battle but also a financial industry, profitable for pharmaceutical companies and even for some doctors who make their living on the suffering of patients. These are sobering realities.

But God's Word speaks a greater reality: **Jesus heals our diseases and sicknesses.** He bore them all upon the Cross. That is not merely a hopeful idea; it is a truth written in Scripture, alive and active today. God's Word is living and breathing, timeless and unchanging, applicable to every generation—past, present, and future. The question for us is this: will we choose to believe it? Will we allow faith in Christ to anchor us more firmly than the facts and fears presented by the world?

This is where faith becomes our lifeline. It is not passive, wishful thinking, but a persistent faith—faith that clings to Christ even when everything else shakes. It is faith that believes God's Word more than the doctor's prognosis. It is faith that overcomes fear and carries us into victory, not because we are strong, but because He is faithful.

Paul speaks in 2 Corinthians 7:6 of how God comforts the downcast, reminding us that He draws near to us in our sorrow. But Paul also warns us to discern the kind of sorrow we carry. Is it worldly sorrow or godly sorrow? Worldly sorrow is a hopeless grief that leads to despair, death in spirit, and separation from God. It feeds depression by whispering lies that nothing will ever change, that hope is lost, and that we are alone. But godly sorrow is different. Godly sorrow brings us back to Him. It leads us to repentance, humility, and renewed trust in the Lord, who loves us.

As caregivers, we must be honest about the depression we feel in the midst of grief. But we must also examine the source of that sorrow. Is it rooted in despair, in listening to the world's report, or in believing the enemy's lies? Or is it a sorrow that drives us to our knees, into the arms of God, where comfort, strength, and healing await?

The difference matters. Worldly sorrow leaves us broken. Godly sorrow draws us closer to our Healer. It is only in Him that our grief is transformed into peace and our depression into hope.

Say this out loud: **I am comforted and encouraged by the One who sees all.**

Now declare this: **I declare that God comforts me in my sorrow and transforms my grief into renewed faith and hope in Him.**

Paul reminds us in this verse that God is the One who comforts the downcast. Caregiving for a loved one with cancer brings moments of deep sorrow, fear, and exhaustion. And depression can feel like an inevitable part of the journey. Yet we are not left to carry this sorrow alone. God draws near to us in our lowest places and lifts us up with His comfort. His presence transforms despair into godly sorrow that leads us back to Him, softening our hearts and renewing our faith. For caregivers, this means we can face grief honestly, while also clinging to the hope that God's comfort is real, personal, and powerful enough to sustain us through every trial.

Prayer of Reflection

Lord, You are the God who comforts the downcast, and today I bring You my sorrow, my grief, and my heavy spirit. Sometimes the weight of caregiving and the fear of cancer feels too much to bear, and depression tries to settle over me like a cloud. But I thank You that You do not leave me in my sorrow. You draw near to me with compassion and lift me up with Your comfort.

Help me, Lord, to discern the difference between worldly sorrow and godly sorrow. When despair tries to take root, remind me that hopelessness does not come from You. Teach me to let my grief drive me into Your arms, not away from You. Let my sorrow become godly sorrow that softens my heart, brings me back to You, and renews my faith.

Cover me with Your peace, strengthen my hope, and remind me that You are present in every tear I cry. Thank You that in my weakness, You are strong, and in my brokenness, You bring healing. I trust You to comfort me and to sustain me each step of this journey. Amen.

Because he has set his love upon Me, therefore will I deliver him; I will set him on high, because he knows and understands My name [has a personal knowledge of My mercy, love, and kindness—trusts and relies on Me, knowing I will never forsake him, no, never]. He shall call upon Me, and I will answer him; I will be with him in trouble, I will deliver him and honor him. With long life will I satisfy him and show him My salvation. Psalm 91:14-16

Psalm 91 is one of my favorite psalms. I try to speak it over my life every day, personalizing it with my own name and pronouns so that God's promises feel close and real. There is something powerful about declaring His Word out loud—it builds faith in our hearts and pushes back against the lies that bombard our spirits.

One of the loudest lies the enemy whispers, especially when we are weary or depressed, is that we are unloved. That, my friend, is a lie straight from the king of liars himself—the devil. The truth is this: God loves us with an everlasting love. He proves His mercy, His kindness, and His protection over and over again. But there is also a response required of us. Psalm 91:14 tells us, *"Because he has set his love upon Me, therefore I will deliver him; I will set him on high, because he has known My name."* When we choose to lean into Him, honor Him, and trust Him, He promises to deliver us and to lift us above the chaos of our circumstances.

As caregivers, we know what it means to be surrounded by troubles. Watching a loved one battle cancer brings daily trials—medical reports, exhaustion, emotions that swing from hope to despair. But here is the good news: these very troubles qualify us for the promises of God. They position us to experience His covering, His refuge, and

53

His faithfulness in ways that go beyond human understanding. He doesn't wait for us to have it all together. He meets us in the middle of our weakness and pours out His strength.

Psalm 91:15 reminds us of another profound truth: *"He shall call upon Me, and I will answer him; I will be with him in trouble; I will deliver him and honor him."* God is not only listening, He is responding. He assures us that when we cry out in the night, when we pour out our fears in prayer, when we feel completely undone, He hears us. Not only does He hear, but He promises to be with us in the trouble. He doesn't stand at a distance and watch us struggle. He walks beside us, He delivers us, and He even honors us in the process.

And then Psalm 91:16 seals the promise with hope: *"With long life I will satisfy him, and show him My salvation."* Satisfaction and salvation are two gifts the world can never provide. For some, "long life" means years added to their days. For others, it means fullness and richness in the days they have left, a deep satisfaction in knowing they are resting in God's will. For all of us, it means the eternal promise of salvation in Christ—a promise that death itself cannot take away.

When we choose to put God first and His Kingdom above everything else, even in the chaos of caregiving, we are setting our love upon Him. And in return, He sets His promises upon us: deliverance, protection, answered prayers, His abiding presence, honor, satisfaction, and salvation. This is the "secret sauce," if you will, of living Psalm 91. It is not just about claiming God's promises, but about responding in love, trust, and obedience to Him in every circumstance.

No diagnosis, no fear, no depression can separate us from the love of God. When we make Him our dwelling place, He becomes our refuge, our fortress, and our unfailing source of help in trouble. And when we call on His name, He answers. He is with us. He delivers us.

He satisfies us with His goodness. And one day, He will show us His salvation in its fullness.

Say this out loud: **I am loved.**

Now declare this: **I declare that because I love the Lord and call on His name, He delivers me, protects me, answers me, and satisfies me with long life and salvation.**

In these verses, God Himself speaks a powerful promise: those who set their love on Him and call upon His name will experience His deliverance, protection, and presence. He promises to answer in times of trouble, to be near in distress, and to bring satisfaction and salvation. For caregivers walking through the uncertainty of cancer, this passage reminds us that our love for God and trust in Him secure His constant care. He does not promise a trouble-free life, but He assures us of His presence in every trial and His victory at the end of the journey.

Prayer of Reflection

Lord, thank You for the promises of Psalm 91. When I feel weak, unloved, or overwhelmed by the weight of caregiving, remind me that those thoughts are lies from the enemy. Your Word declares that You love me with an everlasting love, and I choose today to set my heart upon You.

Help me to dwell in the secret place of Your presence, where I find refuge under the shadow of Your wings. Teach me to put You first in every area of my life, trusting that as I honor You, You will cover me with Your mercy and sustain me with Your strength.

When the trials of cancer and caregiving press in, lift my eyes above the storm and remind me that You are my fortress and my deliverer.

Fill me with peace, steady my spirit, and let my life be a testimony of Your faithfulness. Amen.

Confessions of Grace

For the Lord God is a Sun and Shield; the Lord bestows [present] grace and favor and [future] glory (honor, splendor, and heavenly bliss)! No good thing will He withhold from those who walk uprightly. Psalm 84:11

When a spouse is diagnosed with cancer, Psalm 84:11 can feel almost contradictory to the reality that is unfolding. The verse tells us that the Lord is a sun and shield, that He bestows favor and honor, and that He withholds no good thing from those who walk uprightly. Yet in the midst of hospital visits, difficult treatments, and the fear of losing the one we love, it can be hard to see the good.

But as I reflect on our journey through my husband's cancer, I can now recognize how true this verse really is. God gave us much grace and favor along the way. Even in the darkest of moments, His glory was present. Sometimes it shone like the sun—bright, undeniable, filling us with strength and hope. Other times it felt more like a shield—quiet, steady protection when the fiery darts of fear, doubt, and despair came against us.

There are many fiery darts on the journey of cancer: the enemy's whispers of hopelessness, the weight of depression, the uncertainty of the future. Yet in each of those battles, God's Word proved true. He was our shield when we were weak and our sun when the darkness threatened to overwhelm us. His favor showed up in ways we didn't expect: in the kindness of a caregiver, in the prayers of faithful friends, in the moments of peace that made no earthly sense.

Though the path was painful, I can now see that God did not withhold His goodness from us. His goodness was not defined by the absence of suffering but by His constant presence within it. The favor and honor He bestowed were not worldly rewards, but the deep assurance that we were never walking alone. Even in the valley of cancer, His glory covered us.

Psalm 84:11 is a reminder that God is both our light and our protector. He gives grace for the moment, favor for the journey, and glory for the testimony. Cancer never had the final word—God's goodness did.

Say this out loud: **I have favor and am surrounded by His grace.**
Now declare this: **I declare that the Lord is my sun and shield, and He bestows grace, favor, and glory as I walk with Him.**

Psalm 84:11 reminds us that God Himself is both our sun and our shield. As the sun, He brings light, warmth, and clarity into the darkest seasons of life. As our shield, He protects us from the fiery darts of fear, doubt, and despair. This verse assures us that He bestows grace and favor and that He does not withhold any good thing from those who walk with Him. For caregivers walking through the valley of cancer, this promise may feel hard to grasp in the moment, but it becomes an anchor of hope. God's goodness is not measured by the absence of suffering, but by His faithful presence within it. His favor shows up in small kindnesses, His glory shines even in tears, and His shield surrounds us when we feel weak. In Him, we find both strength for today and the assurance that His goodness will carry us through.

Prayer of Reflection

Lord, thank You for being both my sun and my shield. In the darkness of cancer's shadow, You shine Your light to guide me, and when the fiery darts of fear and despair come against me, You raise Your shield to protect me.

Thank You for the grace and favor You pour out, even in the hardest moments of this journey. I confess that sometimes it is hard to see Your goodness when the pain feels so overwhelming, but I choose to trust Your Word that You do not withhold good from those who walk with You.

Help me to see Your favor in the small moments of kindness, Your glory in the peace that comes unexpectedly, and Your presence in the strength that carries me from one day to the next. Remind me that Your goodness is not absent in suffering, but revealed in Your nearness to me in the midst of it. Let my life and caregiving be a testimony that You are faithful, and that Your love never fails. Amen.

*But He gives us more and more grace [through the pow-
er of the Holy Spirit to defy sin and live an obedi-
ent life that reflects both our faith and our gratitude
for our salvation]. Therefore, it says, "God is opposed
to the proud and haughty, but[continually] gives [the gift
of] grace to the humble [who turn away from self-right-
eousness]. James 4:6*

I remember my pastor telling me when Doug was admitted into
hospice that there would be many people who loved me and who
would surround me in the days, weeks, and months ahead. He said
they would offer me grace, support, and love as I entered the early
days of my widowhood. His words were both comforting and challenging. He told me it would be up to me to accept these gifts—that
I should let people give to me, not turn them away, and not be so
independent that I robbed others of the opportunity to be a blessing.
Instead, I was to humble myself and receive their gestures of love and
care as God's grace extended through them.

And grace did my God give me. In ways I could not have antici-
pated, His grace poured out in those first days and continued in the
weeks and months after Doug's passing. Sometimes it came through
meals left at my door, phone calls from friends who simply wanted
to listen, or cards and letters filled with prayers. At other times, it was
through quiet moments when I felt God Himself whispering peace
to my soul, reminding me that I was not forgotten.

James 4:6 says, *"But He gives more grace. Therefore, He says: God
resists the proud, but gives grace to the humble."* In my grief, I came
to understand the truth of that verse. Pride says, *"I can do this on
my own."* Pride resists help, resists comfort, and resists the hand of

God extended through His people. But humility opens the door to grace—grace that carries, strengthens, and heals.

I discovered that grace often comes wrapped in the love of others. To accept that love is to accept the grace God has appointed for us in our time of need. In my season of widowhood, He showed me again and again that His grace truly is sufficient, and that He gives it freely to those who are willing to receive it.

Say this out loud: **He gives me more and more grace.**

Now declare this: **I declare that God gives me more grace as I humble myself before Him and receive His love through His Spirit and His people.**

James 4:6 reminds us that God's grace is always available in greater measure than our struggles. His grace lifts us in our weakness, comforts us in our grief, and strengthens us when we feel like giving up. But James also makes it clear that this grace flows to the humble, not the proud. Pride insists on carrying everything alone, refusing help from God or others. Humility, however, opens the door to receive God's presence, His provision, and His peace. For caregivers and those navigating grief, this verse serves as a reminder that we don't have to be self-sufficient. God's grace often comes through the hands and hearts of others, and when we humble ourselves enough to accept it, we experience the fullness of His love and strength in our lives.

Prayer of Reflection

Lord, thank You for the promise that You give more grace. In my grief and weakness, I see how much I need that grace every day. Forgive me for the times I've tried to be too independent, too strong in myself, or too proud to accept the help of others. Teach me to humble myself before You and to receive Your grace in whatever form You choose to give it—whether through Your Spirit, through Your Word, or through the love and kindness of those You send into my life.

Help me to see every act of compassion, every prayer spoken over me, and every gesture of support as evidence of Your care. Remind me that accepting help is not weakness but obedience, for You have called us to bear one another's burdens. Thank You, Lord, that Your grace is greater than my pain, greater than my loneliness, and greater than anything I face in this season. Keep me humble, Lord, so that I may never resist Your grace but always live in the overflow of it. Amen.

For it is by free grace (God's unmerited favor) that you are saved (delivered from judgment and made partakers of Christ's salvation) through [your] faith. And this [salvation] is not of yourselves [of your own doing, it came not through your own striving], but it is the gift of God; Ephesians 2:8

In the midst of caring for a loved one with cancer, the line between serving and striving can blur. We often feel as though we must do *more*—pray harder, work longer, or give everything we have—hoping that somehow our effort will turn God's ear toward us or win His favor. Striving can feel like a way to ease the heartbreak that enters a marriage when cancer becomes part of our story. We want to believe that if we can just do enough, maybe we can change the outcome. But striving cannot heal us, and it cannot sustain us.

God's Word in Ephesians 2:8 reminds us of this profound truth: *"For by grace you have been saved through faith, and that not of yourselves; it is the gift of God."* Grace is His unmerited favor, something we cannot earn by our good works, our prayers, or even our deepest sacrifices. Grace is not about what we can do for God but about what He has already done for us through Christ. It is a gift—free, complete, and undeserved.

This truth became deeply personal in my journey. I could not save Doug. As much as I wanted to take away his pain or carry his illness for him, that was never my role to fulfill. Jesus alone could save him. And He did. When Jesus took hold of Doug's heart, Doug surrendered his life fully to Him, and the miracle of salvation became his greatest gift.

So I ask, *can cancer be a gift?* As strange as it may sound, I believe it can. Not because the disease itself is good, it is not, but because God brings treasures out of the ashes. Cancer can become the place where both the afflicted and the caregiver step more deeply into the unmerited favor and free grace that God gives. It strips away our illusions of control, exposes the futility of striving, and invites us to live fully in the grace of God.

Cancer is never something we would choose, yet even in its shadow, God gives gifts: the gift of His presence, the gift of salvation, and the gift of grace that sustains us day by day. His grace is sufficient. His grace saves. His grace carries us through the darkest valleys and assures us that, by faith, His unmerited favor rests upon us now and forever.

Say this out loud: **I am saved.**

Now declare this: **I declare that I am saved by grace through faith, not by my own striving, but by the free gift of God through Jesus Christ.**

Ephesians 2:8 anchors us in a foundational truth: salvation begins and ends with God's grace. It is not a reward for our effort, but a gift we could never earn. For caregivers, this verse offers more than theological clarity; it reorients the heart. When life becomes overwhelming, we often slide into a mindset of spiritual performance, as though God's presence or approval depends on how well we manage the chaos. But Paul's words remind us that grace is not transactional. God's favor does not rise and fall with our strength, our prayers, or our composure.

Grace is rooted in the finished work of Christ, not the shifting conditions of our days. And the same grace that saves us is the grace that steadies us. It meets us in weakness, lifts the pressure to "do it all," and turns our eyes from self-effort to divine sufficiency. Instead of striving, we are invited to rest in the confidence that God's grace is enough for this moment, this season, and every burden we carry.

Prayer of Reflection

Lord, thank You for the gift of Your grace. Your Word reminds me that I am saved by grace through faith—not by my own efforts or striving, but by the finished work of Jesus Christ. Forgive me for the times I have tried to earn Your favor through my good works, my caregiving, or my prayers, as if I could somehow prove myself worthy.

Teach me to rest in the truth that Your grace is a gift—unearned, unmerited, and freely given. Help me release the pressure I put on myself to carry more than You ask of me. Let my heart find peace in knowing that I am loved, accepted, and sustained not because of what I do, but because of who You are.

Thank You for the way Your grace has carried me in caregiving, in grief, and in weakness. Thank You that the same grace that saved me is the grace that strengthens me each day. Lord, let me live not in striving, but in surrender—trusting fully in the gift of Your grace. Amen.

But God's free gift is not at all to be compared to the trespass [His grace is out of all proportion to the fall of man]. For if many died through one man's falling away (his lapse, his offense), much more profusely did God's grace and the free gift [that comes] through the undeserved favor of the one Man Jesus Christ abound and overflow to and for [the benefit of] many. Romans 5:15

Romans 5:15 reminds us that *"the gift is not like the trespass."* The brokenness of sin brought death and despair into this world, but the grace of God through Jesus Christ is far greater—it overflows. Grace does not merely meet us where we are; it surpasses and covers every need, every weakness, and even every moment of anger or despair we face.

Some days, grief and responsibility sat so heavy on my shoulders that even the smallest of routines – breathing, moving, thinking – felt like work. And in the quiet ache of that pressure, a simmering anger arose alongside my exhaustion. Because caregiving isn't just tending to someone you love, it's trying to hold together a whole life while the ground beneath you shifts every day. I was angry at cancer for invading our marriage. Angry at the medical reports that seemed to carry more bad news than good. Angry at the unfairness of watching my husband suffer while I felt helpless to stop it. In those moments, I slipped into striving believing that if I prayed harder, served better, or held everything together perfectly, then somehow God would be obligated to hear me and move.

But that kind of striving only left me exhausted, discouraged, and more broken. What I learned—and am still learning—is that God's grace is not earned through my effort. His favor doesn't depend on my performance. Grace is His gift, freely given through Christ, and it overflows even in the places where I am weak, weary, or angry.

This is the beauty of Romans 5:15: grace is greater. Greater than the trespass of sin, greater than the weight of grief, greater than the brokenness of a cancer diagnosis. Where sin and death entered the world through Adam, grace and life overflow to us through Jesus Christ. That means that even when caregiving feels impossible, even when I fail, even when I feel undone by sorrow and anger, God's grace covers me. It doesn't run out. It doesn't hold back. It overflows.

For caregivers, this truth is a lifeline. We don't have to earn God's presence or prove ourselves worthy of His favor. We simply have to receive the overflowing grace of Jesus. Our role is not to strive, but to surrender to rest in the gift of grace that is greater than every burden we carry.

Say this out loud: **I am sustained through every trial.**

Now declare this: **I declare that the overflowing grace of Jesus Christ is greater than every burden I face, covering my weakness and sustaining me through every trial.**

Romans 5:15 reminds us that while sin brought death and despair into the world through Adam, the gift of God's grace through Jesus Christ is far greater. Grace does not simply meet us at our point of need, it overflows. For caregivers, this truth holds particular significance. Cancer and suffering can stir anger, grief, and feelings of helplessness, yet God's grace is larger than all of it. It covers our weakness, steadies us when we falter, and gives us strength we cannot muster on our own. Where striving leaves us empty, grace fills us. Where sorrow threatens to consume us, grace sustains us. This verse reminds us that we are not left to endure life's burdens in our own strength, but Jesus' gift of overflowing grace is more than enough to carry us through.

Prayer of Reflection

Lord, thank You for the reminder that Your grace is greater than the trespass, and that through Jesus Christ, grace overflows to me. I confess that in the midst of caregiving, I have often felt angry—angry at cancer, angry at the suffering, angry at the weight of a burden I cannot control. At times, I have tried to strive my way into Your favor, believing that if I prayed harder or worked more, You would hear me differently.

But Your Word tells me the truth: Your grace is not earned; it is a gift. It is not fragile or scarce, it overflows. Thank You that Your grace covers my anger, my exhaustion, and even my failures. Thank You that what Adam's sin brought into this world, Your Son has overcome with life, mercy, and healing.

Help me, Lord, to stop striving and instead surrender to the gift of Your grace. Teach me to receive it daily, to rest in it when my heart feels weak, and to rely on it when my spirit feels undone. Let Your overflowing grace fill the broken places in me, sustain me through the demands of caregiving, and remind me that Your love is always greater. Amen.

Confessions of Fear and Despair

Yes, though I walk through the [deep, sunless] valley of the shadow of death, I will fear or dread no evil, for You are with me; Your rod [to protect] and Your staff [to guide], they comfort me. Psalm 23:4

When my father was dying in 2015, Psalm 23 became my anchor. I whispered its words over and over as I sat beside him, drawing comfort and reassurance from the promise that the Lord is our Shepherd and that even in the valley of the shadow of death, we are not alone. Those memories of caring for my father came flooding back years later as I sat by Doug's bedside in our local hospice facility.

The care and attention Doug was receiving there filled me with both gratitude and sorrow. I realized how much I had struggled to provide for him at home in those final days. I had tried to do it all myself—holding on tightly, trying to be strong, determined to meet every need—but in my humanity, I fell short. Though I did the best I could, I now understood how uncomfortable and restless he must have been as I tried to navigate the unknown terrain of dying and letting go.

With tears streaming down my face, I whispered apologies to him—telling him I was sorry for what I didn't know, for what I couldn't do. I knew he could still hear me; research tells us that hearing is often the last sense to fade. But beyond science, I simply *felt* that he could hear me. My heart was aching with regret, and in that vulnerable place, the enemy tried to whisper lies of failure into my spirit. He wanted me to believe I hadn't done enough—that I had failed my husband when it mattered most.

But God.

In that quiet space, the Lord reminded me to lift my eyes off the natural and fix them on the eternal. He gently whispered that He was walking beside me, just as He always had. He was the same Shepherd who had comforted me when my father passed, and He was the same Shepherd now leading me through this valley. His presence filled the room, not with explanations, but with peace. I sensed His rod and His staff, His authority and His guidance, steadying me and keeping me from sinking under the weight of grief.

The world around me felt sunless and heavy with shadows. I was walking through the lowest valley I had ever known. Though I understood that we are all appointed to die and return to our Creator, my heart could not accept that Doug's time with me was drawing to a close. It felt unbearable to imagine life without him. Yet, in those sacred final breaths, God's comfort broke through my disbelief and despair.

I knew then what David meant when he said, *"I will fear no evil, for You are with me."* Even as I faced death's shadow, God's presence filled the space between heaven and earth. He comforted me in the way only He could. And in that moment—amid tears, love, and loss—I knew I would never walk alone again.

Say this out loud: **I am not alone on my journey.**

Now declare this: **I declare that even in the darkest valleys of caregiving and grief, the Lord is with me; His presence comforts, strengthens, and sustains me.**

Psalm 23:4 reminds us that even when we walk through the darkest valleys—the valleys of suffering, caregiving, and loss—we are never alone. God's presence goes before us, beside us, and behind us. For the caregiver, this truth becomes deeply personal. The long nights, the exhaustion, the fear of what's coming next—these moments can feel like living in the shadow of death. Yet, in that very place, God's comfort becomes tangible. His rod represents His authority and protection; His staff represents His care and guidance. Together they remind us that His love is active, not distant. We don't have to fear what lies ahead because our Shepherd walks with us, guiding us gently through the pain into His peace. Even in grief, His presence brings light to the darkness, strength to the weary, and the promise that we will never walk alone.

Prayer of Reflection

Lord, You are my Shepherd, and even in the darkest valleys of caregiving and grief, You are with me. When the shadow of death loomed over my husband's life and my own heart trembled with fear, You never left my side. You comforted me when I could not comfort myself. You steadied my spirit when the weight of sorrow was more than I could bear.

Forgive me, Lord, for the moments when I believed the enemy's lies that I had failed, or that my love was not enough. Remind me that You were present in every prayer I whispered, in every act of care I offered, and in every tear that fell. You were the strength behind my hands, the peace in my heart, and the mercy that filled the room when I felt completely undone.

Teach me to see caregiving not as a measure of perfection but as a holy partnership with You—one where my weakness becomes the space for Your grace to flow. Help me release the guilt, the what-ifs, and the regrets, trusting that Your rod and Your staff guided both of us every step of the way.

Even now, Lord, as I walk through grief, let Your presence be the light that leads me out of the shadows. Comfort me as only You can and remind me that I will never walk alone—for You are, and always will be, my Shepherd. Amen.

There is no fear in love [dread does not exist], but full-grown (complete, perfect) love turns fear outdoors and expels every trace of terror! For fear brings with it the thought of punishment, and [so] he who is afraid has not reached the full maturity of love [is not yet grown into love's complete perfection]. 1 John 4:18

Doug was resting more and more as his strength faded. He had rallied several times for family visits, but that evening, he was tired. The soft glow of dusk filtered through the window as I stood by his bedside, tears spilling freely from my eyes. I just needed him to hold me—to feel the safety and love that had carried us through forty years together. Little did I know that this would be one of the last hugs he would ever give me.

Our daughter was visiting with her little girl, and though we didn't always agree with some of her choices, we were thankful she had come to spend time with her dad. Still, tension lingered beneath the surface. One afternoon, words were exchanged that cut deeply—old hurts, unmet expectations, and unspoken pain all bubbled over into accusations and tears. I was undone—emotionally, spiritually, and mentally. Instead of grace and understanding, I felt attacked at one of the most vulnerable moments of my life.

My heart was shattered. I longed for my husband's comfort, for his steady reassurance and quiet strength. I needed him to hold me and remind me that everything was going to be okay—that we were still united in love and purpose despite the storm swirling around us.

I fell onto his chest, sobbing, "Please don't leave me yet."

He gently rubbed my back and whispered, "Not yet. I'm still here. It's going to be all right. You're a good wife and a good mom. She'll leave soon, and it'll be the two of us again for a while before my sister gets here."

In that sacred moment, I felt the fear and despair melt away in the warmth of his love. The chaos of the day gave way to stillness. His words, his touch, and his unshakable calm enveloped me like a cloak of peace. I realized that this—this love—was stronger than fear, stronger than death, stronger than anything we faced.

That night, perfect love truly did cast out fear. The legacy we had built over four decades—our laughter, our faith, our family—paled in comparison to the perfect, holy love that flowed between us in that moment. It was a glimpse of God's own love: steadfast, patient, and full of grace.

Say this out loud: **I am loved.**

Now declare this: **I declare that God's perfect love drives out all fear from my heart, filling me with His peace, confidence, and unshakable assurance of His presence.**

1 John 4:18 reminds us that fear cannot coexist with perfect love. Fear thrives in uncertainty, but true, God-given love brings peace, security, and confidence in the One who holds our future. For the wife and caregiver, fear often takes many forms: fear of the unknown, fear of loss, fear of not being enough. Yet God's Word teaches us that His perfect love drives out every trace of fear. When we abide in Him, His love becomes the antidote to the anxiety that tries to consume us. In caregiving, we see this truth lived out daily. The selfless love that moves us to care, comfort, and remain steadfast in suffering is a reflection of God's own heart. His love doesn't ignore pain—it transforms it. It meets us in the middle of our heartbreak and reminds us that even in loss, love remains. Perfect love doesn't deny fear's

existence—it overcomes it, one act of grace, one whispered prayer, and one moment of surrender at a time.

Prayer of Reflection

Heavenly Father, Thank You for the gift of perfect love, the kind of love that casts out fear and steadies my trembling heart. In moments when emotions overwhelm me, when fear, grief, and conflict swirl around me, remind me that Your love is my anchor.

Lord, I confess that sometimes I have tried to carry too much on my own. I have let fear whisper that I am not enough— not strong enough, not loving enough, not faithful enough. But You, Lord, remind me that I don't have to be perfect, because Your love is.

Teach me to rest in that perfect love. Let it fill every aching place in my soul where fear once lived. When sorrow grips me, wrap me in Your peace. When my heart feels divided, unite it again in Your truth. When I am weary from caregiving and loss, let Your love be the steady rhythm that carries me through each day.

Thank You, Jesus, for showing me what perfect love looks like through Your sacrifice and through the quiet, steadfast love shared between husband and wife. Help me to reflect that love to others, even when my heart is broken. May Your perfect love continue to cast out all fear, until all that remains is peace.

In Jesus' name, Amen.

But even in case you should suffer for the sake of right-eousness, [you are] blessed (happy, to be envied). Do not dread or be afraid of their threats, nor be disturbed [by their opposition]. 1 Peter 3:14

Doug had the misfortune of being diagnosed with stage 4 lung cancer during the height of the COVID-19 pandemic. The world was gripped by fear, but as people of faith, we chose to stand firm in our convictions and not take the vaccine. At the time, we didn't realize how that single decision would add an extra layer of challenge to his already difficult cancer journey.

I remember distinctly the chemical oncologist's words—spoken not once, but repeatedly like a curse over my husband's life. Each week at Doug's appointments, he would say, *"You know, Doug, if you get COVID, it will kill you."* It was as if death itself had been invited into the room with those words. Finally, I had had enough. I looked him squarely in the eyes and said, *"We don't speak death over my husband. Please don't say that again."*

Fear was running rampant in the world, and unfortunately, that same fear had infiltrated the medical field. The turning point came when Doug suffered a severe allergic reaction to immunotherapy. A treatment I had been hesitant about from the beginning but had agreed to because it was ultimately Doug's decision. I could see he was reacting badly, but when I voiced my concern, the nurses dismissed me. *"It sounds like COVID,"* they insisted. *"Take him to the emergency room."*

Every instinct within me screamed *no.* I knew that a trip to the ER, especially during that time, could very well be a death sentence for him. Instead, I leaned into the Holy Spirit's guidance, and we turned to homeopathic and natural remedies. By God's grace, Doug pulled through that terrifying episode and he lived for three more precious years after that.

Looking back, I can see how fear had tried to infiltrate my mind and weaken my resolve. I'd like to say that I was always steadfast and unshakable, but I am human. The enemy knows how to whisper lies into our vulnerabilities especially when we are weary and afraid. Yet God's Word reminds us to take *every* thought captive, to measure it against His truth, and to keep our eyes fixed on Him.

1 Peter 3:14 reminds us that when we suffer for doing what is right, we are blessed. Choosing faith over fear, truth over intimidation, and trust in God over dependence on man's systems—these are not easy paths. But they are the paths that lead to peace. We were not called to live under fear, but to walk boldly in the confidence that God is our defender and sustainer.

When the world speaks fear, we speak faith. When others see death, we see life. And when the voices around us declare impossibility, we stand on the Word that says all things are possible through Him who believes.

Say this out loud: **I am unafraid.**

Now declare this: **I will not fear what others fear, for the Lord is my protector and peace; even in suffering, I am blessed because His presence surrounds me and His truth sustains me.**

Caregiving through a spouse's battle with cancer often places us face-to-face with fear — fear of the diagnosis, fear of decisions, fear of loss. During Doug's illness, that fear was amplified by the world's own panic during the pandemic. Yet Scripture reminds us that even when we suffer for doing what is right, we are blessed. God's presence stands as our shield when others' words or actions stir anxiety or doubt. As caregivers, we must remember that fear is not our portion. We are not to be intimidated by the opinions of the world or the grim reports of men, but to anchor ourselves in God's unchanging promises. He calls us to walk in courage, not because the battle isn't real, but because *He* is with us in it. Faith does not ignore reality — it looks beyond it to the One who rules over every outcome.

Prayer of Reflection

Heavenly Father, in moments when fear rises like a flood and the world's voices grow louder than Your truth, quiet my soul to hear only You. When I feel pressured to conform, remind me that my trust belongs solely to You. Give me discernment to recognize fear for what it is — a thief of peace — and the courage to stand firm in faith.

Lord, You know the weight of caregiving, the uncertainty of test results, and the exhaustion of endless decisions. I surrender my worries to You, knowing that You are my defender, my wisdom, and my strength. Help me to choose faith over fear, truth over lies, and peace over panic. Let my life, and the way I walk through this journey, be a testimony of Your love and power. In Jesus' name, Amen.

Fear not [there is nothing to fear], for I am with you; do not look around you in terror and be dismayed, for I am your God. I will strengthen and harden you to difficulties, yes, I will help you; yes, I will hold you up and retain you with My [victorious] right hand of rightness and justice.
Isaiah 41:10

Seeing Doug lying so still and peaceful in his hospice bed brought me no comfort. My heart was torn in two as I sat beside him, realizing that the man I loved, my best friend and husband of over forty years, was slipping away. I was terrified of the future — of the silence that would fill the spaces he once occupied, of waking up alone, of making decisions by myself. I wasn't sure how I would go on without him.

Everyone told me how strong I was, how brave and composed I seemed, but inside, I was crumbling. My thoughts were tangled in fear and grief. I questioned everything — my identity, my purpose, and my ability to survive what was coming. The weight of it all pressed down on me like an invisible burden, and I buckled under it. I kept asking God, *Where is the rightness in this?* We were supposed to grow old together. What happened to the dream of celebrating our fiftieth anniversary, surrounded by our children, grandchildren, and maybe even great-grandchildren? Those dreams vanished like smoke before my eyes.

My heart hardened with sorrow as I faced the reality that I would soon be a widow — a word that felt foreign, unwanted, and heavy. I had married at eighteen, just six weeks after high school. I had never lived on my own, never paid a mortgage alone, never eaten dinner at a table set for one. I wasn't sure I could start now. The thought of living in a quiet home with only the dog for company filled me with dread.

And yet, even in that darkness, I had to keep functioning. I had to find the strength I didn't feel. I smiled and expressed my gratitude to the hospice nurses and aides who cared for Doug and me so tenderly. I tried to be strong for our children and grandchildren, who were navigating their own waves of grief. Inside, I felt empty and selfish for wanting more time, more years, more life together. I felt barren — stripped of the life we had built and terrified of the future that awaited me.

But then came the whisper of Isaiah 41:10: *"Fear not, for I am with you."* Those words were like oxygen to my suffocating soul. I realized that I wasn't facing the future alone, not really. God was still with me. He hadn't abandoned me in my grief. He was there, upholding me with His righteous right hand, giving me the strength I lacked and the courage to face what was ahead.

In that moment, I began to see that His strength would carry me when mine was gone. His hand would guide me when I couldn't see the way forward. And His presence — steadfast, patient, and loving — would remind me that though I had lost my earthly companion, I was not alone.

Say this out loud: **I am not alone.**

Now declare this: **I will not fear the future, for my God is with me; He strengthens me, helps me, and upholds me with His righteous right hand.**

Caregiving and grief often strip us to our core, revealing our deepest fears and frailties. When faced with the loss of a spouse, it's easy to feel alone, abandoned, and unsure of how to move forward. Yet Isaiah 41:10 reminds us that fear has no power where God's presence abides. He promises to be our strength when we have none, our help when we can't carry the load, and our support when we can barely stand. In the midst of widowhood, loneliness, or uncertainty, God doesn't just tell us to be strong — He becomes our strength. His righteous right hand lifts us from despair and steadies us in every trembling step. We do not walk this road alone; His presence is our constant companion, and His love our sustaining force.

Prayer of Reflection

Heavenly Father, when fear grips my heart and the weight of loss feels unbearable, remind me that I am never alone. You are my strength when I am weak, my help when I cannot help myself, and my peace when my world feels uncertain. Thank You for holding me with Your righteous right hand and carrying me through the valley of grief

Lord, I surrender my fears about the future into Your loving care. Teach me to trust that Your plans for me still hold hope and purpose, even when I can't yet see them. When loneliness creeps in, draw me close to Your presence. When sorrow overtakes me, breathe Your comfort over my weary soul. Thank You that You are my God — steady, faithful, and true — and that Your strength will always be enough for me. In Jesus' name, Amen.

The fear of man brings a snare, but whoever leans on, trusts in, and puts his confidence in the Lord is safe and set on high. Proverbs 29:25

When someone you love is diagnosed with cancer, fear sets in almost instantly. It's as if the very word *cancer* has its own power — summoning dread, anxiety, and a thousand "what ifs." The world has given cancer a throne, calling it the "big one," the monster that steals lives and hope. And if we're not careful, that fear begins to take root in our hearts, whispering lies louder than God's promises.

From the very beginning of Doug's diagnosis, we chose to trust God and hold onto the truth that *He would work all things together for our good because we loved Him (Romans 8:28).* But I would be lying if I said that fear didn't sometimes feel bigger than our faith. There were moments — long, quiet nights in the dark — when the "what ifs" seemed to outweigh the "but God."

Fear became a snare in our lives for a time. Without realizing it, we began to give it a seat at the table. When talking about plans or the future, Doug and I would often say, *"But he has cancer,"* as though that single fact had the authority to determine the course of our days. Every doctor's visit, every insurance form, every hospital check-in required us to speak it aloud — *cancer* — over and over again, reinforcing its place in our story. I often felt that was a trap laid by the enemy, a way to keep us focused on the disease rather than on the Healer.

For a season, God gave us a gift, a time of remission, a reprieve from the storm. In that space of calm, we rediscovered joy and purpose. We learned to live again without the constant shadow of the diagnosis. We learned to worship in peace rather than in panic. But then, like a sudden windstorm, the cancer returned stronger, faster, spreading like wildfire through Doug's body.

The truth of how far it had advanced didn't hit us until that day in the hospital, when swelling in Doug's brain revealed what was really happening beneath the surface. The doctors said it was a rare side effect of radiation and though we caught it early, it shook our family to the core. Both of our sons rushed to the hospital to be with us. One of them, a war veteran, had seen his share of pain and death; he stood by me, steady and focused, helping me make decisions and ask the hard questions. Our younger son struggled more deeply, overwhelmed by the sight of his strong father so frail and suffering. It was a breaking moment for all of us.

And yet, through all the chaos, through all the fear, God remained our anchor. He did not remove the storm, but He calmed our spirits within it. We leaned into Him more deeply than ever before, trusting that He was still writing our story, still holding our lives in His hands.

Proverbs 29:25 reminds us that fear itself is the trap, the snare that steals peace and blinds us to God's faithfulness. But those who trust in the Lord are kept safe. Not safe from pain or loss, but safe in His love, in His purpose, and in His presence. Fear isolates, but faith anchors. And in the end, the safety we found wasn't in doctors, test results, or even temporary healing — it was in the unshakable truth that God was with us in every breath, every battle, and every heartbreak.

Say this out loud: **God is with me.**

Now declare this: **I refuse to be trapped by fear; I place my full trust in the Lord, who keeps me safe and steady through every storm.**

The fear that often comes with a cancer diagnosis can quietly become a trap — one that binds our hearts, limits our faith, and clouds our view of God's goodness. Proverbs 29:25 reminds us that fear is not just an emotion; it is a snare designed by the enemy to pull our focus away from the One who holds the power of life and healing. As caregivers and spouses, it's natural to feel the weight of fear pressing in from all sides — from medical reports, statistics, or even our own thoughts. But God's Word calls us to shift our focus from what threatens us to Who sustains us. Trust in the Lord is the antidote to fear's poison. When we place our confidence in Him, we find safety not in outcomes, but in His unchanging presence. In every unknown, every setback, every sleepless night, He is our refuge.

Prayer of Reflection

Heavenly Father, fear so often creeps in quietly through the doctor's words, through the stillness of the night, through the heaviness of what I see before me. It tries to bind me, to steal my peace, and to convince me that cancer or loss has the final say. But Lord, I know that You are greater. You have not given me a spirit of fear, but of power, love, and a sound mind.

Today, I choose to trust You above every report, every statistic, and every anxious thought. You are my refuge and my protector. When fear tries to entangle me, help me remember that I am safe in Your hands. Let my faith rise higher than my fear, and let my heart rest in the truth that You are always working for my good.

Lord, remind me that no diagnosis, no circumstance, and no darkness can overpower Your light. My confidence is not in what I see, but in Who You are — faithful, loving, and true. Thank You for being my shelter and my steady place when the storms rage. I rest in Your peace. In Jesus' name. Amen.

He shall not be afraid of evil tidings; his heart is firmly fixed, trusting (leaning on and being confident) in the Lord. His heart is established and steady, he will not be afraid while he waits to see his desire established upon his adversaries. Psalm 112:7-8

What I love about these verses is the phrase, *"his heart is established and steady."* Those words are a promise and a challenge because staying established and steady when the world is shaking beneath you takes supernatural strength.

How does one remain steady in the face of a cancer diagnosis; in the whirlwind of fear, doctor visits, uncertainty, and loss? The answer doesn't come from our own strength; it comes from a surrendered heart that clings to God's promises, even when every emotion screams otherwise.

When we become believers in Jesus Christ, we begin a lifelong journey of transformation. Paul reminds us to "be transformed by the renewing of your mind" (Romans 12:2). For a cancer-fighting wife, that transformation means choosing every day to renew your mind in God's truth instead of the world's fear. It means dismantling strongholds one by one; the fear of the unknown, the fear of cancer itself, the fear of being alone, the fear of not being enough for the battle ahead, the fear of what others think, and the fear of a future that feels uncertain.

The truth is, none of us is promised an easy path in this life. Even for those who love God deeply, there will be trials that shake us to our core. The enemy's intent is clear — to steal, kill, and destroy. And cancer does just that. It destroys routines, dreams, and sometimes the very rhythm of family life. It forces a wife to become a nurse, a decision-maker, and eventually, a widow. It dismantles what was and leaves behind a reality we never wanted to have.

But God in His mercy and love calls us to be *established and steady* in the midst of that destruction. He anchors our hearts when everything else feels untethered. His Word tells us that His thoughts are higher than ours and His plans greater than we can imagine. Even when life feels like rubble, He is still building something beautiful from the ashes.

As I step into this season of widowhood, I am learning that being steady doesn't mean being emotionless. It doesn't mean pretending to be strong all the time. It means being rooted deeply in the One who is unshakable. My stability is no longer found in marriage, security, or plans; it is found in my relationship with God, my true Husband, who covers me with His peace and holds me when I crumble.

I cry out to Him often and He hears me. When the grief swells, His presence steadies me. When fear whispers, His love silences it. When I don't know how to take the next step, He gently leads me forward. That is what it means for my heart to be *established and steady* — not that I don't feel the pain, but that I am not defined by it.

God has proven that He is my rock, my fortress, and my steady foundation. He is the same yesterday, today, and forever even when everything else changes.

Say this out loud: **God is my steady and sure foundation.**

Now declare this: **My heart is established and steady, trusting in the Lord who silences fear and secures me in His unfailing love.**

Fear thrives in uncertainty. For those caring for a loved one with cancer or walking through the valley of loss afterward fear often feels constant. Yet Psalm 112 reminds us that the one who trusts in the Lord can live with a heart that is *fixed*, *established*, and *steady*. This kind of strength doesn't come from willpower or emotional control; it comes from surrender. When our hearts are anchored in God's promises, we can face even the hardest news without being overtaken by dread. To be "established" is to be rooted in His unchanging character — to know that even when life unravels, God remains faithful. When our emotions waver, His Word steadies us. When fear rises, His peace reigns. The faithful heart learns not to deny the pain but to stand firm in the presence of the One who holds it all together.

Prayer of Reflection

Heavenly Father, You see every tremor of fear in my heart and every anxious thought that stirs within me. You know how easily I can become shaken by circumstances beyond my control. Yet You promise that the one who trusts in You will not be afraid. Lord, help my heart to be established and steady in You.

When the doctor's report brings discouragement, when loneliness whispers that I am forgotten, when the weight of grief feels too heavy, remind me that I am held by You. Let Your peace take root where fear once lived. Strengthen me to walk forward each day, not in my own resolve, but in the quiet confidence that You are with me.

Thank You for being my steady place, my anchor, and my faithful foundation. Teach me to rest in Your promises and to keep my heart fixed on You — unshaken, unafraid, and unwavering in faith. In Jesus' name, Amen.

Be angry [at sin—at immorality, at injustice, at ungodly behavior], yet do not sin; do not let your anger [cause you shame, nor allow it to] last until the sun goes down. And do not give the devil an opportunity [to lead you into sin by holding a grudge, or nurturing anger, or harboring resentment, or cultivating bitterness]. Ephesians 4:26-27

My breath came in gasps. I was so angry at Doug. The pressure of caregiving had finally pushed me past my breaking point. I was slamming dresser drawers, shoving clothes into a suitcase, ready to leave. I told myself I was done. I couldn't take one more sarcastic comment, one more heavy silence, one more reminder that our life together had turned into an endless cycle of appointments, medications, and fatigue.

This wasn't supposed to be my life.

I called my friend to let her know I was almost packed. She had invited me to stay the night—probably hoping a little distance would cool the storm brewing inside me. But before I could leave, I realized both sets of car keys were missing. Doug had hidden them.

"You aren't taking either of my cars," he said firmly. "You'll have to find another way to get where you think you're going."

His words ignited a fresh wave of fury. He had all the control over the vehicles, over the house, and, in that moment, it felt like he had control over *me*. I screamed in frustration, angry at him, at cancer, at myself. The voice in my head whispered what I feared most: *You are nothing without him.*

But then came the tears. I crumpled under the weight of my own emotions, called my friend back, and said I wouldn't be coming after all. I unpacked my suitcase, got a glass of water, and whispered a weary, "Good night." I wasn't going anywhere.

That night, I cried out to God for help. I knew I hadn't handled the situation well. I had let anger and despair take the driver's seat. But even in the mess of it all, God's gentle presence met me there. I began to see that Doug's words had come from his own fear and pain. Cancer was stealing from both of us and sometimes, it tried to take our compassion too.

The next morning, we discussed openly what had happened. I told him how hurt and trapped I had felt. He shared his fear of losing control, of being dependent, of watching me wear out. There were tears, but later that day, we laughed at something silly on TV.

We learned not to let the argument fester. Love, humility, and forgiveness became our healing balm. After forty-one years of marriage, we still had things to learn but the most important lesson of all was that our unity was stronger than any disease. Cancer didn't like a united front. We leaned into our covenant, our vow before God, to love each other until death do us part.

Say out loud: **I will walk in unity, forgiveness, and love.**

Now declare this: **Even in my anger and exhaustion, I will not let bitterness take root. I choose to surrender my emotions to God, allowing His peace to guard my heart and mind. I will walk in unity, forgiveness, and love.**

Ephesians 4:26–27 reminds us that anger itself is not a sin—it's what we do with it that matters. "Be angry and do not sin," Paul wrote, warning believers not to let anger linger or give the devil a foothold. This scripture came alive for me the night I reached my breaking point as a caregiver. I had allowed frustration, exhaustion, and hurt to drive my emotions, and in doing so, I opened the door for bitterness to enter my heart.

But the next morning, when Doug and I humbled ourselves and talked through the hurt, healing began to flow. This passage taught me that even righteous emotions must be surrendered quickly to God before they harden into resentment. As caregivers, we will experience anger at the situation, at the disease, even at the person we love but through confession, forgiveness, and humility, God turns our anger into an opportunity for grace. When we lay our emotions before Him, He restores peace, unity, and love, closing the door that the enemy tries so hard to pry open.

Prayer of Reflection

Heavenly Father, You know the depth of my exhaustion and the sharp edges of my emotions. Sometimes, the weight of caregiving feels too heavy to carry, and anger rises within me. Forgive me, Lord, when I let frustration speak louder than love.

Teach me to pause before I react, to breathe before I speak, and to listen for Your voice in the middle of my storms. Help me remember that my spouse is not the enemy—sickness and fear are. Cover our home with Your peace, Lord. Let Your Spirit guard our words, our hearts, and our unity.

When anger knocks, remind me of Your grace. When despair settles in, remind me of Your presence. Thank you for loving me through every emotion and for never letting go. In Jesus' Name, Amen.

Confessions of Courage

And this is the confidence (the assurance, the privilege of boldness) which we have in Him: [we are sure] that if we ask anything (make any request) according to His will (in agreement with His own plan), He listens to and hears us.
1 John 5:14

"She said, *'I'm amazed at your courage and calmness.'*

I had to chuckle, because inside I felt nothing but turmoil. My faith felt like it was faltering, and honestly, I wasn't even sure I wanted to have this conversation. Part of me wanted to hang up the phone and avoid talking about the grief and exhaustion that came with caregiving day after day.

She had once served the Lord, but now she spoke more of "the universe" and "mother nature" than of the King of Kings. My heart ached for her. I could see how her trials had made her more anxious and bitter, while she looked at me and saw courage and calmness. *If only she knew.*

"All God," I said simply. "Without Him, I'd be nothing more than a puddle on the floor from all the tears I've cried in the quiet places." She laughed, perhaps not fully grasping the depth of what I meant. I knew her questions weren't meant to hurt, but her callousness toward the difficult journey Doug and I were navigating pierced my spirit. Still, I kept steering the conversation back to faith, sensing that's what the Lord wanted me to do.

I didn't feel bold. In fact, I felt small and uncertain. Isn't someone strong in faith supposed to articulate clearly where their strength comes from, to testify boldly in the middle of the storm? That's what I thought, yet all I had was a trembling heart and a simple truth: my strength came from God alone.

Eventually, she shifted into her own struggles, unloading complaint after complaint about the latest crisis in her life. I sat quietly, listening, realizing that what she really longed for was to feel heard. In that moment, I recognized a mirror of my own heart. I, too, had stumbled in my belief at times, wondering if God was really listening to me, if He truly heard the cries of my heart.

So, I set aside my own grief and questions, choosing to listen. And as I listened, I offered words of reassurance. I reminded her that things would work out, that there was still hope in her situation and in mine as well. It wasn't eloquent or polished, but it was honest. And maybe, in the end, that's what courage and calmness really look like: not having it all together but pointing back to the One who does.

Say this out loud: **He listens and hears me when I call to Him.**
Now declare this: **I declare that I can approach God with confidence, knowing that He hears me when I pray according to His will.**

John reminds us that prayer is not a desperate cry into the void but a confident conversation with our Heavenly Father. When we pray according to His will, we can rest assured that He not only hears us but is already at work. This truth gives us courage to bring our needs, grief, and desires before Him, trusting that His answers are always rooted in love and aligned with His perfect plan.

Prayer of Reflection

Lord, You know how weak and weary I feel. Others may see courage and calmness in me, but you see the truth of my heart—the tears I cry in secret, the doubts that whisper, and the weight of grief I carry. Thank You that I don't have to be strong on my own, because Your grace is enough for me.

Even when I stumble in faith, You steady me. Even when my words feel inadequate, Your Spirit speaks through me. Thank You for reminding me that weakness is not failure, but the very place where Your power shines brightest. Help me to keep pointing others back to You, even when I feel empty. And when I wonder if You hear me, remind me that You are always listening, always present, always near.

Be my courage, my calmness, and my strength today and every day. Amen.

*Be strong, courageous, and firm; fear not nor be in terror
before them, for it is the Lord your God Who goes with you;
He will not fail you or forsake you. Deuteronomy 31:6*

I realized that the more I helped my husband in his fight against cancer, the stronger and more courageous I became, even when I didn't feel either of those qualities inside myself. Day after day, as I stood beside him in the battle, I discovered a strength that wasn't my own and a courage that only God could supply.

It reminds me of the story of the three young Hebrew boys (Shadrach, Meshach, and Abednego) who refused to bow to the king's idol and were thrown into the fiery furnace. They did not stand there because they felt brave; they stood there because they trusted in the God who promised to be with them. And when the flames rose around them, the king himself looked and saw a fourth figure walking in the fire—One who looked like the Son of God.

That's exactly what it felt like in my own furnace of suffering. I didn't feel strong, but God gave me strength. I didn't feel courageous, but He wrapped me in His courage. And just like those three young men, I was never alone in the fire. Jesus was with me, walking through the flames of cancer, caregiving, and grief.

The truth is this: we don't have to feel brave to live courageously. We only have to cling to the God who promises to never leave us nor forsake us. His presence turns weakness into strength and fear into courage, moment by moment, breath by breath.

Say this out loud: **I am strong and courageous.**

Now declare this: **I declare that I will not be afraid or discouraged, for the Lord my God goes with me and will never leave me nor forsake me.**

This verse reminds us that we are never alone, no matter how overwhelming the battle feels. God Himself goes before us, walks beside us, and remains with us. His presence gives us courage when our hearts tremble and strength when we feel weak. We can face uncertainty, grief, and every trial with confidence, because the Lord has promised that He will never leave us nor forsake us.

Prayer of Reflection

Lord, I thank You that just as You were with Shadrach, Meshach, and Abednego in the fiery furnace, You were with me in the fire of cancer and grief. I did not always feel strong or courageous, but You gave me the strength I needed to care for Doug and to keep walking forward. You never left my side, even when the flames of sorrow and fear felt overwhelming.

Now, as I grieve the loss of my husband, I ask You to continue to walk with me through this fire. Remind me that I am not alone, and that Your presence is my courage. Teach me to trust You in the hardest moments, when my heart feels faint and my spirit weary. May Your power be made perfect in my weakness, and may my life reflect the hope and faithfulness of the One who never abandons His children.

Thank You for being my Comforter in grief, my Strength in weakness, and my Companion in the fire. Amen.

Be strong and courageous. Be not afraid or dismayed before the king of Assyria and all the horde that is with him, for there is Another with us greater than [all those] with him. With him is an arm of flesh, but with us is the Lord our God to help us and to fight our battles. And the people relied on the words of Hezekiah, king of Judah. 2 Chronicles 32:7-8

While reading this scripture during my quiet prayer time, the word "horde" stood out to me. It felt painfully accurate, because Doug and I seemed to be fighting an uphill battle—ill-equipped, outnumbered, and unprepared—for the horde of negativity we so often faced from his medical providers.

At that time, Doug was struggling badly with hydration. I was alarmed, more than I wanted to admit, that he might not survive long enough for the kids and his siblings to come and say their goodbyes. I didn't know what to do. Every step I tried to take felt blocked, every path forward obstructed. I felt outmaneuvered by the enemy, outstrategized at every turn, and I couldn't see how Doug and I could recover, even to the fragile baseline of health he had managed to maintain for the last several months.

That evening, I took our dog, Spot, for a walk in the field beside our apartment building. While I watched him roam, I sat with my phone pressed to my ear, waiting on hold with the oncology answering service for the doctor on call. My heart raced with worry.

Finally, she answered.

"I'm concerned that he is dehydrated," I told her, "and he's deteriorating to the point where I may need to take him to the ER."

Her voice was forthright, blunt, even a little cold. "Describe his symptoms to me," she said. After I did, she replied with a certainty that cut through me: eventually, Doug would reach a point of no return, and there would be no winning this battle.

Her words stung like arrows. How could I, a believer in Jesus Christ, come to terms with such blunt negativity? How was I supposed to walk back into our apartment, look Doug in the eyes, and ask him to push a little longer—go to the ER, get fluids, fight for more time? Would he allow me to help prolong his life, or was he already as tired and weary of the battle as I was?

In that moment, my spirit sank. I felt hopeless. I felt angry—not only at the disease that was robbing us, but at the doctor's clinical frankness that left no room for hope. And worst of all, I didn't feel God's presence. I didn't feel His help. It was as if the heavens were silent while I stood in the field, tears burning my eyes, clutching a phone in one hand and Spot's leash in the other.

Looking back, I see that grief and exhaustion had blinded me. God had not abandoned me in that moment; He was still walking with me in the field, still whispering strength even when I could not feel it. But in that raw space of fear and fatigue, I only felt the weight of the horde pressing in around me.

Say this out loud: **I am not alone in my battles.**

Now declare this: **I declare that I will not be afraid of the weight of grief, for the Lord fights for me and gives me strength beyond my own.**

Hezekiah encouraged the people not to fear their powerful enemy, reminding them that human strength is limited, but God's power is limitless. In the same way, when we walk through grief and suffering, we may feel small and overwhelmed by the weight of sorrow. Yet we are not left to face it in our own strength. The Lord fights for us, upholds us, and surrounds us with His presence. Our comfort comes in knowing that though grief feels like a mighty enemy, God is far greater, and His strength will carry us through.

Prayer of Reflection

Lord, You know how heavy that night felt, when fear, exhaustion, and hopelessness pressed in like a horde. I didn't feel Your presence, and I didn't hear Your voice. I only felt the silence, the weight of decisions I didn't know how to make, and the pain of watching Doug decline. Yet even when I couldn't sense You, You were there.

Thank You for being faithful in the moments when my faith falters. Thank You that Your strength holds me when my own is gone, and that Your hope endures even when my heart feels hopeless. Teach me to trust that You are near, even in the silence. Give me courage to face hard conversations, wisdom to know when to speak and when to be still, and peace to rest in Your care for both Doug and me.

When I feel surrounded by the horde, remind me that I am never truly alone. You are my refuge, my strength, and my ever-present help in trouble. Amen.

Act like men and be courageous; grow in strength! 1 Corinthians 16:13

We had received the devastating news early on: Doug's cancer had already spread to his brain. That was what made it stage 4. Without the brain involvement, it would have been classified as stage 2, and according to medical science, his odds of survival would have been much higher. But instead, we were thrust immediately into the harshest reality of the diagnosis.

And yet, we were believing for a miracle. God was strengthening our faith day by day, teaching us to surrender to His purposes in this season of our lives. We held tightly to the truth that He was with us, even in the face of medical charts and grim statistics.

Doug had just completed his first radiation treatment to the brain, and I went to pick him up from the oncology clinic. He explained to me what the process had been like. Before the treatment, a custom mask had been molded to fit tightly over his face and head. The mask was then strapped securely to the treatment table so that he could not move even an inch. Once in place, the technicians slid him into the machine that would deliver focused beams of radiation directly to the spots where the cancer had taken root.

Doug told me how precise the calculations had to be that the technicians used their skill, knowledge, and even math formulas to make sure the radiation struck the cancer and not healthy brain tissue. The restraint, the mask, the immobilization, they all served one purpose: to protect him even as they fought to kill what was attacking him.

When he came out of the clinic, I could see the weariness in his body. As he got into the car, I asked softly, "How was it?"

He leaned back in the seat, gave me a faint smile, and said, "Let's go home. It was interesting, but I think I can handle it."

I looked at him with admiration and said, "You're the bravest guy I know."

The truth was, I wasn't sure if I could have done what he was making seem like "no big deal." To me, the thought of being strapped down, face covered, unable to move, while beams of radiation pulsed into my brain was terrifying. But to him, it was just another step in the fight. He was so strong and fearless in my eyes, even when I knew he was tired.

And in that moment, what he wanted more than anything was not to analyze the treatment or dwell on the diagnosis. He just wanted to go home, sink into his chair, watch a western, and rest.

Say this out loud: **My faith is strengthened day by day.**

Now declare this: **I declare that I will stand firm in my faith, staying watchful, courageous, and strong through the power of Christ.**

Paul urges believers to stay alert, to stand firm in the faith, and to be strong and courageous. For those navigating caregiving or grief, this reminder is especially poignant. Life's trials can drain our strength and shake our resolve, but God calls us to lean on Him as our source of courage. To "stand firm" does not mean we never stumble: it means we keep anchoring ourselves in Christ, trusting His strength when ours is gone. Even in the valley of loss, we can remain watchful for His presence, courageous in His promises, and strong in His sustaining grace.

Prayer of Reflection

Lord, there are times when life places us in situations that feel overwhelming and frightening. In those moments, we long to run, yet we find ourselves held still by circumstances we cannot change. Thank You that even then, You are present and at work.

Teach us to trust that when we feel restrained or powerless, it is not without purpose. Just as a steady hand can protect and guide, so You steady our hearts so that Your healing love can reach the deepest places of our souls.

When fear rises, give us courage. When weariness sets in, grant us rest. And when we cannot see the outcome, remind us that Your purposes are good and that You will carry us through. Thank You for being our Comforter, our Healer, and our anchor in the storm. Amen.

But instantly He spoke to them, saying, Take courage! I Am! Stop being afraid! Matthew 14:27

I was sitting quietly in the ICU waiting room, trying to hold my peace in the middle of so much uncertainty. Soft praise music played through my headphones as I opened my Bible and searched for healing scriptures. With my journal open, I began writing down verse after verse, speaking each one over Doug as an act of faith.

Doug was in surgery. His radiation oncologist had determined that the best treatment at this stage of his disease was a lung ablation for the tumor that had returned. After almost eighteen months of remission, the cancer had come back. The PET scan revealed the tumor glowing brightly, and his doctor suspected that it was beginning to grow again. Because of Doug's weakened condition, surgery to remove his lung was no longer an option; the doctor had warned that such a procedure would almost certainly take his life. Ablation was the only path forward.

As I sat waiting, I prayed earnestly for the surgeon's hands, for the assistants and nurses, and for every detail of Doug's care. Doug himself had accepted the risks with his characteristic optimism. He believed, as I did, that this might finally beat back the beast of cancer once and for all.

I was lost in scripture and prayer when I suddenly looked up to see the surgeon and his assistant standing before me. My heart skipped a beat as I turned down the music, closed my Bible, and prepared to hear the news.

The doctor smiled slightly as he gave his report. He was optimistic. He explained that he had successfully obliterated the tumor and that Doug's lung had sealed properly after the procedure. Still, Doug would need to spend two nights in the hospital to recover, and because of his history of a heart attack, he would be placed overnight on the cardiac floor as a precaution.

Relief washed over me. I thanked the doctor sincerely, but more than that, I praised God right there in the waiting room. I even shared a brief word of faith with the surgeon, acknowledging that while medicine had done its part, we ultimately trusted in the One who heals.

Quickly, I gathered up my Bible and journal, my companions in the waiting, and hurried toward recovery so I could see my husband. Each step was filled with gratitude that God had once again carried us through the fire, giving us more time together.

Say this out loud: **I do not face the storms of life alone.**

Now declare this: **I declare that I will not be afraid, for Jesus is with me, and His presence gives me courage and peace**.

Jesus calls out to His disciples as they tremble in fear, assuring them of His presence and telling them to take courage. In the same way, when we face the storms of grief or the overwhelming demands of caregiving, His voice speaks into our fear. Courage doesn't come from our own strength but from the assurance that Jesus is with us. His presence calms our hearts, quiets our fears, and gives us peace even when the storm continues to rage.

Prayer of Reflection

Lord Jesus, when fear rises and the storms of life surround me, help me to hear Your voice above the noise: *"Take courage! It is I. Don't be afraid."* Thank You that I do not face grief, loss, or uncertainty alone. You are with me in every moment. Calm my anxious heart with Your peace, strengthen me with Your courage, and remind me that Your presence is greater than any storm. Teach me to rest in the assurance that You are near, and that with You by my side, I have nothing to fear. Amen.

Wait and hope for and expect the Lord; be brave and of good courage and let your heart be stout and enduring. Yes, wait for and hope for and expect the Lord. Psalm 27:14

Usually, the time between Doug's scans and the results was about a week, sometimes even longer. That period of waiting, the "in-between", was always its own lesson. Each time, I tried to hold onto hope that the scan would show remission again, or at least some shrinkage of the tumors and lesions.

During the summer of 2023, Doug and I traveled back to Lake Erie, where we had grown up, met, fallen in love, and gotten married. It was meant to be a sentimental trip, a chance to reconnect with family and the places where our story began. But Doug was in increasing pain. His neck bothered him terribly, and it only seemed to worsen each day. He blamed it on a freak accident, jamming his neck while driving a tractor through his family's grape vineyards. He was convinced that once we got home and he saw his chiropractor, things would improve.

But in my spirit, I sensed something deeper was wrong. I kept those fears to myself, choosing instead to speak words of encouragement: "Once we're home, we'll get it fixed." Yet as the days passed, I could see the toll it was taking on him. Doug had an incredibly high pain tolerance, but this pain was different. He slept more, grew more irritable, and carried himself with the heaviness of someone in constant discomfort. My brave warrior was struggling, and my heart knew it.

When the doctor entered the exam room after Doug's latest scan, his face carried none of his usual warmth. My heart sank.

"We have a problem," he said plainly. "It looks like the cancer has spread to the bone. There's a large cancerous lesion on C-3 in your neck. That explains the pain you've been having."

Doug nodded silently, as if to confirm what he already knew in his body. I gathered my courage and asked the question that always followed: "What is the course of treatment?"

"Radiation," the doctor replied.

I swallowed hard. "Will he need to have a mask made?"

"Yes. And it looks like there's also a small lesion on the brain, so we'll target both areas. I'm also prescribing a stronger pain medication. Bone cancer is extremely painful, and honestly, I'm surprised you've managed as well as you have up to this point."

I reached for Doug's hand as we left the clinic, holding it tightly in mine. Once again, we were stepping into another season of waiting—waiting for radiation, waiting for results, waiting for God to move. Yet in the middle of it all, we carried our expectation of the Lord. We prayed, we believed, and we continued to hope for His miracle of healing, trusting that even in the darkest valleys, He was still with us.

Say this out loud: **I am brave and stout in heart.**

Now declare this: **I declare that I will wait for the Lord with courage, trusting that He will strengthen my heart as I place my hope in Him.**

This verse calls us to wait on the Lord with courage and trust, even when life feels unbearable or uncertain. Waiting is not passive; it is an act of faith that anchors us in God's timing rather than our own. In seasons of grief, when our hearts feel faint and the future unclear, His strength sustains us. As we place our hope in Him, we learn that the waiting itself becomes a place where God renews our courage and deepens our trust.

Prayer of Reflection

Lord, waiting is hard when my heart is heavy with grief and my spirit longs for relief. Yet Your Word reminds me to wait for You with courage, trusting that You will strengthen my heart. Teach me to rest in Your timing, even when I cannot see what lies ahead. When I feel weary, be my strength; when I feel afraid, be my courage; when I feel empty, be my hope. Help me to believe that as I wait on You, You are working all things for good, and that joy will rise again in Your perfect time. Amen.

Confessions of Health and Healing

O Lord my God, I cried to You and You have healed me.
Psalm 30:2

I had been keeping a secret.

I wasn't feeling well. My body felt inflamed, I was exhausted all the time, and every joint ached. I didn't want to burden Doug with my own health challenges while he was fighting so hard against his. But I should have known better. All Doug ever had to do was look at me, and he could see straight through.

"So, when are you going to the doctor? I can tell you aren't feeling well," he said one evening.

At that, I burst into tears. And you know what? It's okay to cry in the midst of the battle.

We were on our 40th anniversary trip to Chautauqua County, New York, the place where we had grown up, met, and married. For us, the idea of "vacation" was always different than most. We didn't plan cruises or exotic destinations. Instead, we made long treks across the country to see our family, visit relatives, and immerse ourselves in the familiarity of home.

For years, I had dreamed that maybe, just maybe, we would finally take a real honeymoon after forty years of marriage. However, instead, our anniversary trip was spent on his family's farm, where we stayed in the old homestead where Doug had grown up. We had planned to stay for several months, but life and circumstances beyond our control cut our stay short. In the end, we only stayed seven weeks.

Through tears, I finally admitted, "I'm going to make an appointment when we get home. I promise."

I want to be honest with you, my reader: caregiving is a demanding and challenging job. It is exhausting. It drains you physically, emotionally, and spiritually. Not only are we contending for our husband's healing, but sometimes we are fighting our own battles in the background. For me, it was the ongoing struggles of menopause—aches, fatigue, and emotions that seemed out of my control. I felt overwhelmed, like life was spiraling in every direction.

And that's the crux of it, isn't it? When is it necessary for caregivers to prioritize their own health and well-being? The answer is simple: when we realize that we cannot pour from an empty vessel. The mark of a wise caregiver is the ability to recognize when self-care is needed. Yes, we are called to care for our husbands with love and devotion, but we must also remember that God has entrusted us with our own bodies, minds, and spirits. A breakthrough in caregiving often comes when we finally recognize that caring for ourselves is part of caring for them.

Psalm 30:5 reminds us, *"Weeping may endure for a night, but joy comes in the morning."* David declares that God's favor lasts a lifetime. The truth is that the battles we face are not merely physical; they are spiritual in nature. And the way we tap into God's sustaining power is through faith—believing in our hearts and speaking that belief with our mouths.

Paul puts it beautifully in 2 Corinthians 4 when he says that the treasure of the gospel, the power of salvation and life, is from God, not from ourselves. He acknowledges the tension we live in: *"We are hard pressed on every side, but not crushed; perplexed, but not in despair."* As caregivers, that verse often feels like it was written just for us.

Sister in Christ, when we face the most overwhelming circumstances, when our bodies ache, when our strength runs low, when our emotions feel fragile, we can rest in this truth: God hears our cries. He heals us as caregivers, and He sustains us as we walk beside our husbands in their sickness. The power of life comes from God, and even in the midst of cancer, the life of Jesus shines through our fragile, weary bodies.

Say this out loud: **God hears me and heals me.**

Now declare this: **I am blessed because I know in my spirit that God hears me when I call upon Him. He heals every disease in my body. My mind is transformed daily by His Word. He never fails to hear me and heal me. He is always faithful to His covenant with me. He brings joy in the morning and wipes every one of my tears.**

Refuse to be double-minded in acknowledging that God hears you and heals you. Open up a conversation with God about your body, soul, and spirit, and how He wants to heal you in all those areas. Rest in the peace He brings to every situation for you and for your husband. He hears and knows it all. He isn't surprised by one thing that happens in your life. Turn to Him and trust in the fact that He hears you when you cry out to Him in your distress.

Prayer of Reflection

Lord, You see the weight I carry as I care for my husband, and You know the toll it takes on my body, my mind, and my spirit. Thank You that I do not have to hide my weakness from You. When I feel exhausted, inflamed, or broken, You are my strength and my healer.

Teach me to recognize when I need rest and care, and remind me that taking care of myself is not selfish, but rather part of how You equip me to serve my family well. Thank You for the promise that weeping may endure for a night, but joy comes in the morning. Help me to cling to that truth when the nights feel long and overwhelming.

Even when I am pressed on every side, I trust that I am not crushed. Even when I am perplexed, I know I am not in despair. Your power sustains me, and Your Spirit breathes life into my weary soul. Be my Comfort, my Healer, and my Joy as I walk this journey with You. Amen.

Beloved, I pray that you may prosper in every way and [that your body] may keep well, even as [I know] your soul keeps well and prospers. 3 John 2

"You read it. You know I don't know any of those medical terms." On May 25, 2021, we received the diagnosis that would change everything. I burst into tears as the weight of the words sank in. Doug sat quietly beside me, his face etched with disbelief. Due to the bureaucracy of the VA healthcare system, we didn't even hear the news directly from a doctor. We had to request the results ourselves.

There we were, sitting in the sanctuary of our living room, scrolling through the report, stumbling over unfamiliar words, and searching the internet to piece together what they meant. We were left to interpret devastating medical language without compassion, guidance, or hope. Eventually, after I called to complain, an intern phoned us. She spoke bluntly, with no warmth, her English broken and her tone detached. Instead of offering comfort, she left us feeling even more frustrated and angry at the system that had failed us in such a personal moment.

I remember thinking, *"How could this attack on Doug's health possibly prosper us in every way"*? At that time, nothing about this diagnosis looked or felt like prosperity.

And yet, as I look back, I see now how God's prosperity is not measured by medical outcomes or earthly ease. Even in uncertainty and illness, He was shaping us, sustaining us, and teaching us.

God prospered us in ways we didn't expect. We built new relationships with medical professionals, some of whom cared deeply, while others challenged our patience and persistence. In those encounters, we had opportunities to share our faith. Against the odds, even in the face of negative reports and difficult appointments, we testified that our hope was in God and that we believed in His healing power. Our spiritual roots grew deeper as we leaned harder on Him.

For Doug, the journey became one of renewal. He recommitted his heart to God, growing beyond a distant belief into a daily fellowship with the King of Kings. He called his prayer time his "going apart" time, often spending hours walking along the North Platte River with Spot, his loyal companion, by his side. Those walks were sacred meetings where Doug poured out his heart and drew strength for the fight.

We found that as we put God first in everything, we prospered, even in the good, the bad, and the ugly. Our prayer life flourished. Our faith matured. We encouraged other patients sitting in oncology waiting rooms and hospital lobbies, offering words of hope to those who also carried heavy diagnoses. We discovered that prosperity wasn't about life going the way we wanted; it was about God walking with us through every moment, shaping our hearts, and revealing His nearness.

Through tears, setbacks, and victories, we learned this unshakable truth: in all things, God's plan is better than anything we could have imagined. And we knew beyond any doubt that Jesus was walking right alongside us on the cancer journey, steady, faithful, and present in it all.

Say this out loud: **God prospers me in every way. He keeps my body and soul well.**

Now declare this: **I declare that it is God's will for me to prosper and be in good health, even as my soul prospers in Him.**

John expresses his heartfelt prayer that believers would experience health and prosperity in every area of life, just as their souls flourish in Christ. It reminds us that God cares not only about our spiritual well-being but also about our physical, emotional, and practical needs. True prosperity is found in the balance of a healthy soul and a life surrendered to God's care.

Prayer of Reflection

Lord, thank You that You care about every part of me; my body, my mind, and my soul. In the midst of caregiving and grief, I often neglect my own health and feel the weight of exhaustion pressing in. Yet Your Word reminds me that it is Your desire for me to prosper and be in good health, even as my soul prospers in You.

Teach me to find balance between caring for others and caring for myself. Restore my strength where I am weary, heal my body where it is weak, and renew my soul in Your presence. May my life reflect the wholeness that only You can bring, and may I trust You to provide for every need, physical, emotional, and spiritual. Amen.

Heal me, O Lord, and I shall be healed; save me, and I shall be saved, for You are my praise. Jeremiah 17:14

The knock on the passenger-side window of our car startled me.

Doug jumped, his whole body tensing. By this point, his central nervous system had taken a hit from all the treatments, and his fight-or-flight response was heightened far beyond normal. He pressed the button and rolled down the window.

Standing there was a woman we recognized from the oncology center's waiting room. She leaned in gently and asked Doug if she could pray for him. We nodded, and right there in the parking lot, she began to pray with boldness and compassion. She not only prayed over him but also prophesied, encouraging him to begin praying out of the Psalms, speaking God's Word directly over his body and circumstances.

Her words felt like a divine appointment. We thanked her, blessed her for her obedience to God's prompting, and then made our way home.

Later that day, I sat down with my Bible and journal, compiling a list of Psalms that we could declare together. Doug and I began to speak those scriptures aloud over his body. As we prayed and praised, our spirits began to lift. A new sense of joy emerged in our daily lives, one that was not dependent on medical reports or outcomes, but rooted in God's presence and His promises.

Were we perfect about it? No. We didn't manage to recite those scriptures every single day. But the power was not in our perfection—the power was in God meeting us in our desperation. Each time we turned to Him in faith, He answered with comfort, strength, and renewed hope.

What began as a startling knock on a car window became a holy reminder that God is always near, always ready to encourage us through the obedience of His people and the power of His Word.

Say this out loud: **You are the One I praise!**
Now declare this: **I declare that the Lord is my healer and my praise, and in Him I am saved and made whole.**

Jeremiah cries out to God as the only true source of healing and salvation. It reminds us that when we are broken in body, heart, or spirit, our help does not come from ourselves or others but from the Lord alone. As we place our trust in Him, He not only restores us but also becomes the focus of our praise, even in the midst of our struggles.

Prayer of Reflection

Lord, You are my healer and my salvation. In my grief and brokenness, I come to You just as Jeremiah did, asking You to restore me. My heart feels weary, my spirit wounded, and yet I know that only in You can I find true healing.

Thank You that Your power reaches deeper than my pain and that Your presence is greater than my sorrow. Teach me to trust You with the wounds I cannot fix, and let my life become a testimony of Your saving grace. Even as I walk through loss, may my lips continue to praise You, for You alone are my hope and my wholeness. Amen.

Is anyone among you sick? He should call in the church elders (the spiritual guides). And they should pray over him, anointing him with oil in the Lord's name. And the prayer [that is] of faith will save him who is sick, and the Lord will restore him; and if he has committed sins, he will be forgiven. James 5:14-15

Spot alerted us to visitors in the hallway of our apartment building. At first, he barked, but then his tail began wagging furiously, as if even he knew something special was about to happen.

Several elders from our church had come to pray for Doug. They entered our small apartment with love and reverence, carrying the presence of God with them. Toni held a prayer cloth in her hands—a simple piece of fabric that had been prayed over by the visiting evangelist who was in town for a crusade meeting. To us, it wasn't just a cloth; it was a tangible reminder of faith, prayer, and the connection of the body of Christ.

One by one, the elders laid hands on Doug and me. They spoke life over us, declaring God's promises with boldness. They anointed Doug with oil, just as Scripture teaches, and prayed fervently for his healing. Their voices were strong, yet tender, calling on the Lord to pour out His mercy, His peace, and His strength into our weary hearts.

As they prayed, I could feel the heaviness of illness begin to lift from the atmosphere of our tiny home. It was as though the prayers themselves pushed back the darkness and invited the light of God's presence to flood every corner of the room.

Marilyn, one of the elders, embraced me with tears in her eyes. She held me close as though to carry part of my burden on her own shoulders. Through my own tears, I whispered, "Thank you so much for coming today. It's going to be okay. We are surrendered to His peace."

Doug sat quietly, but I could see the calm in his face. He knew he was saved. He knew the Lord was his healer. It was settled in his mind, and there was no doubt in his heart. The prayers of our brothers and sisters didn't just comfort us; they strengthened our faith, reminding us that we were not walking this road alone.

When the last "Amen" was spoken and the elders departed, our home felt different. The peace of God rested in every room. Doug and I looked at one another, not with despair, but with a renewed sense of hope. All was well, not because the cancer had disappeared in that moment, but because the Lord was present, and His peace was enough to sustain us.

Say this out loud: **I am saved from illness and restored in Him.**
Now declare this: **I declare that through prayer in faith and the anointing of the Lord, I receive His healing, restoration, and forgiveness.**

After healing the man at Bethesda, Jesus later found him and reminded him to turn from sin so that nothing worse would happen to him. The man then went and testified to the Jews that it was Jesus who had healed him. These verses demonstrate that healing encompasses not only the physical body but also the spiritual or emotional aspects of the soul. Jesus calls us to live in holiness after we have received His mercy, and our response should be to give Him glory by sharing what He has done for us.

Prayer of Reflection

Lord Jesus, thank You for being the One who heals not only my body but also my soul. Just as You called the man at Bethesda to walk in newness of life, help me to live each day in obedience to You. Guard me from returning to old patterns of sin or fear, and instead fill me with Your Spirit so that my life gives testimony to Your mercy. May my healing—whether physical, emotional, or spiritual—become a witness that points others to You, the true Healer and Savior. Amen.

*He heals the brokenhearted and binds up their wounds
[curing their pains and their sorrows]. Psalm 147:3*

The physical pain of cancer is beyond description.

My husband had always been a beast of strength: athletic, power-ful, and determined. To watch that same man become debilitated, his life measured by the timing of his pain medication, was almost unbearable. It broke my heart to see him suffer not only from the pain itself but also from the endless side effects as the cancer spread throughout his body and into his brain.

I often cried out to the Lord with desperation: *"Heal Doug's wounds, Lord. Ease his pain. Bring relief to the man I love."* There were days when all I could do was weep and pray, asking God to pour mercy over him.

And yet, out of the pain and darkness, beauty and peace would sometimes break through. When Doug fixed his gaze on Jesus, when his attention shifted from the disease to the Savior, something mirac-ulous happened. The pain became more tolerable, his spirit settled, and moments of joy returned. He could focus again, smile again, even enjoy small slices of life in the midst of the battle.

God did cure his pain, not always in the way we hoped for, but through His presence, His comfort, and His peace. He was faithful to walk with us in sorrow and to carry us when our strength failed.

I came to see that focusing on Jesus brought health to more than just our bodies. It bound up our wounds, soothed our minds, and steadied our hearts. Healing came not only through medicine but through faith in action, through prayer, worship, Scripture, and sur-render. As we chose to turn our attention toward Him, we received life even in the shadow of death.

What the enemy meant for destruction, God used to draw us closer to Himself. And in that nearness, we found the strength to keep going, one day at a time.

Say this out loud: **I am saved from illness and restored in Him.** Now declare this: **The Lord heals my broken heart and binds up my wounds with His love.**

God tenderly cares for those who are hurting. He does not overlook our pain but moves toward us in compassion, bringing healing to our broken hearts and binding up the wounds that life and loss have left behind. It reminds us that no sorrow is too deep for His comfort, and no wound is beyond His power to heal.

Prayer of Reflection

Lord, You see the places in my heart that are broken, the wounds that no one else can touch. Thank You for being the God who heals and the One who binds up every hurt with Your gentle hands. In my grief and sorrow, remind me that I am not forgotten or alone. Bring Your healing to the cracks in my spirit and restore my hope with Your love. Teach me to trust Your timing and Your care as You mend what feels shattered within me. Amen.

For I will restore health to you, and I will heal your wounds, says the Lord, because they have called you an outcast, saying, This is Zion, whom no one seeks after and for whom no one cares! Jeremiah 30:17

I see myself as a cancer-fighting wife, and that is why I chose it as the title of this devotional. The journey of caregiving has left me with scars of brokenness—emotional, physical, and spiritual. Those scars tell the story of sleepless nights, countless doctor visits, hard conversations, and the quiet tears I cried when no one else was watching.

Through it all, my only anchor was God. He was the one constant when everything else felt uncertain. He is always faithful and true. His promises never waver, and His Word never fails. What He says He will do, He does—though sometimes not in the way I expect or in the timing I would choose.

My testimony of God's faithfulness can become your testimony too. If you find yourself in the hard, hidden places of caregiving—places of exhaustion, grief, or fear—know this: you are not alone. The same God who carried me will carry you. The same God who steadied me in weakness will strengthen you. When you anchor your heart in Him, you will discover a peace that surpasses understanding and a hope that endures even in the darkest valleys.

Caregiving is not a role anyone asks for, but it becomes holy ground when we walk it with the Lord. And in Him, we find the courage to fight, the grace to endure, and the strength to keep loving through the brokenness.

He hears our cries for relief. He cares for our mourning. He sees our brokenness.

Say this out loud: **I am restored to health. I am not abandoned by my God.**

Now declare this: **He will restore me to health and heal my wounds.**

God promises to restore health and heal wounds, speaking hope to a people who feels abandoned and broken. It reminds us that no matter how deep our pain or how lasting our scars, God's power to heal reaches every part of our lives—body, heart, and spirit. His restoration is not only physical but also emotional and spiritual, bringing wholeness where we feel shattered.

Prayer of Reflection

Lord, I hold tightly to Your promise that You restore health and heal wounds. You see the places in my life that feel broken from caregiving, grief, and loss. You know the pain that lingers in my body and the ache that weighs on my heart. Thank You that You are the God who restores, the Healer who binds up what no one else can reach.

Teach me to trust Your healing work, even when it comes little by little and not all at once. Help me to believe that nothing in my life is too damaged for You to redeem. Restore my strength, renew my joy, and bring wholeness to my spirit. Let my healing become a testimony of Your love and faithfulness, bringing hope to others who walk this same path. Amen.

Confessions of Grief

Jesus said to her, I am [Myself] the Resurrection and the Life. Whoever believes in (adheres to, trusts in, and relies on) Me, although he may die, yet he shall live; John 11:25

About one week before he went unconscious, Doug looked at me and said with a seriousness in his voice, *"I'm afraid my time here is short."*

I couldn't bear to think about that possibility, so I redirected our conversation and tried to speak life into our situation. I wasn't ready for him to leave me. In my heart, I kept thinking selfishly that if he could just hold on until I turned sixty, I would be better taken care of because then I could collect his Social Security and not have to worry so much about finances and my own security after he was gone. I placed my hope in timelines and milestones, convincing myself that maybe he would live past March, or even into April, so we could celebrate my 60th birthday and his 70th together.

I had even told the grandkids about my plan for a "130th Party," where we would celebrate our milestone birthdays together. They laughed and enthusiastically agreed that it would happen, and for a moment, that dream gave us something lighthearted to hold on to.

But Doug saw things more clearly than I did. He looked at me tenderly and said, *"You know, you will be fine when I'm gone. Maybe even relieved that you won't have to take care of me anymore."*

Tears filled my eyes as I responded, *"I won't be fine if you aren't here. I love you, and I don't want to do life without you."*

He reached over, held my hand, and in that quiet, sacred moment, we didn't speak of it again. A week later, he slipped into unconsciousness and began an eleven-day stay under hospice care.

And now, here I am—learning how to "do life" without him. The ache of his absence is real, and at times it feels unbearable. Yet, *but God*. In His mercy, He has sustained me step by step. Even in the moments when I no longer wanted to live without Doug, God met me with a peace that truly surpasses all human understanding.

He became my strength, my comfort, and even my Husband—just as He promised to be for widows (Isaiah 54:5). What I thought would be the end of my story became the beginning of a new journey with Him.

Say this out loud: **I will live and not die.**

Now declare this: **I declare that Jesus is the resurrection and the life. Because I believe in Him, I will live even if I die, and His life and power are at work in me today and for eternity.**

In John 11:25, Jesus reveals one of the greatest truths of the gospel: *He Himself is the resurrection and the life.* Resurrection is not just an event in the future—it is a person, Jesus Christ. By believing in Him, we are given eternal life that transcends physical death. For the believer, death is not the end but a doorway into everlasting life with God. This verse calls us to put our hope, not in our own strength or the things of this world, but in Christ alone, who holds the power over both life and death. That is our eternal hope in the fight against cancer.

Prayer of Reflection

Lord Jesus, You are the resurrection and the life. In You, death has been defeated, and eternal life is secure. When grief weighs heavily on my heart and fear of loss presses in, remind me that You hold the keys of life and death. Help me to rest in the promise that those who believe in You will live, even though they die. Fill me with the hope of reunion with my loved ones in Your presence, and give me strength to walk in Your resurrection power today. Amen.

*Blessed and enviably happy [with a happiness produced
by the experience of God's favor and especially conditioned
by the revelation of His matchless grace] are those who
mourn, for they shall be comforted! Matthew 5:4*

As our friends began arriving at the church for the funeral, I felt
like a fraud. My heart pounded with the weight of the moment, and
I wasn't sure how I could possibly hold myself together to eulogize
Doug. The thought of standing before everyone, sharing the memories our children and grandchildren carried of their beloved Dad and
Papa, felt almost unbearable.

Sweat gathered on my palms, and a wave of panic rose within me
as we stood waiting to greet those who came to honor his life. Yet in
that very moment, God's grace began to meet me. Inch by inch, His
comfort settled over me like a warm blanket, steadying my trembling
heart. What seemed impossible in my own strength became possible
because of His presence.

I realized that God had given me the favor and the strength I
needed not only to speak words that honored Doug's life and our
love, but also to mourn openly and truthfully the loss of the man
who had been my companion for forty-one years. Even as the tears
flowed, a quiet joy rose in my soul. I rejoiced in knowing that Doug
was now with his Lord and Savior, free from pain and suffering, and
that one day I would see him again in glory.

In that sacred space where grief and hope intertwined, I was
strengthened. God gently reminded me of the family Doug and I had
built together, the children and grandchildren who carry his legacy
into the future. With God's help, I could embrace the calling to be
the best mother and grandmother I could be, continuing to nurture

the family we had cherished, and passing down the love that Doug and I shared into the generations yet to come.

Say this out loud: **I am blessed and comforted in my mourning and grief.**

Now declare this: **I am filled with a happiness that is produced by my experience of God's favor and grace in the current situation of grief. I am not alone. He walks with me and comforts me while I mourn. I am blessed. I am favored. I am comforted. Grief will not win!**

Jesus assures us that God sees and honors our grief. Mourning is not a place of abandonment but a place where His comfort meets us. Those who mourn can find blessing in the nearness of God, who promises to bring peace, healing, and hope in the midst of sorrow.

Prayer of Reflection

Lord, You see my tears and know the depth of my sorrow. Thank You for promising comfort to those who mourn. When my heart feels heavy and my spirit weary, remind me that I am not abandoned but held close by You. Wrap me in Your peace that goes beyond understanding, and help me to trust that joy will return in Your timing. Teach me to rest in Your presence, where true comfort and healing are found. Amen.

The Lord is close to those who are of a broken heart and saves such as are crushed with sorrow for sin and are humbly and thoroughly penitent. Psalm 34:18

The view of the funeral home across the parking lot from where I sit in the city's best Mediterranean restaurant feels humbling and surreal. An emptiness settles over me, mingled with a deep sense of aloneness, as I watch the city continue on as if nothing has happened. Cars pass, people laugh, conversations carry on, yet only a few hours ago, my husband died, and the world seems utterly unchanged.

My stomach growls as the waitress sets a beet and feta salad in front of me. She has no idea that my last meal was more than twenty-four hours earlier. With a cheerful smile, she asks if there is anything else I need. My first thought is to tell her the truth—that what I need is my husband back—but instead, I swallow the ache, force a polite smile, and simply thank her for the food.

I bow my head, whispering thanks for the meal before me, but more importantly for God's comfort that is holding me up when nothing else can. A few tears slip down my face as I take my first bite. The flavors of the salad fill my mouth, but my heart tastes only grief. It feels shattered, and I cannot imagine when—or if—it will ever feel whole again.

Yes, I know that Doug is with Jesus, safe and free from suffering, and for that I rejoice. But that truth doesn't change the reality that I am sitting here alone in this restaurant, staring across at the funeral home that now holds the body of the man I love. The world rushes on, unaware, but I sit in the quiet tension of grief and faith, clinging to the God who promises to be near to the brokenhearted.

Say this out loud: **I am not alone.**

Now declare this: **The Lord is close to me when my heart is broken, and He rescues me when my spirit feels crushed.**

God's nearness is revealed to those who are hurting, assuring us that He does not stand far off in times of grief or despair. When our hearts are broken and our spirits feel crushed under the weight of life's struggles, God leans in with compassion and offers His comforting presence. Rather than dismissing our pain, He meets us in it. He always brings comfort, strength, and hope. Our brokenness draws Him near to us, rather than pushing Him away. His closeness brings rescue and healing from our grief.

Prayer of Reflection

Father, Your Word says that You are near to the brokenhearted and that You save those who are crushed in spirit. Today, I bring you my broken heart. The loss of my husband feels unbearable, and at times, the weight of grief threatens to overwhelm me. Yet I choose to trust Your promise that You are close, even in this valley of sorrow. Wrap me in Your presence when the loneliness feels too heavy. Remind me that I am not abandoned, but held by Your everlasting arms. Heal my wounded heart little by little, and give me the courage to keep walking forward until the day when every tear will be wiped away. Amen.

For His anger is but for a moment, but His favor is for a lifetime or in His favor is life. Weeping may endure for a night, but joy comes in the morning. Psalm 30:5

I had arrived in New York for the family gathering to celebrate Doug's life just two weeks earlier. Yes, I was weepy, but I felt as though I had a handle on the waves of grief that kept pressing against me. Having walked through the death of my father nine years ago, I was no stranger to grief. I had spent years in counseling and gathered many tools to help me cope, and I thought I was equipped to face this final milestone of 2024.

And then I took a shower.

Without warning, the sobbing began. I couldn't stop. Wave after wave of grief crashed against my heart, relentless and unending. I was staying at Doug's family farm, living in the very house he had grown up in, lovingly called "the homestead" by his sister. Surrounded by his memory, I felt undone. As the hot water ran over me, the tears gave way to wailing, and lament poured out of me. I didn't just cry the tears; I gave them a voice. I cried out to God with all my fear and sorrow, begging for His presence and His help.

My heart was overwhelmed with more than grief. I worried about finances and the uncertainty of my future. I carried the deep pain of my daughter severing contact with me just a week before her father's funeral. I felt battered by strained and complicated relationships, not only within Doug's family but also my own. Their lack of empathy for my sudden widowhood pierced me even deeper. Every side of my life seemed to be pressing in at once, and I could see no joy ahead—only emptiness. In that moment of despair, I told God through my tears and wailing that I was utterly ill-equipped to handle what was expected of me, let alone what He might expect of me.

Yet in the middle of all the chaos, a gentle truth broke through the noise of my anguish. Over and over again, I heard the words: *"Joy comes in the morning."*

And as always, God was right.

By the next morning, the storm had lifted. The heaviness loosened its grip, and I could breathe again. The sadness and intense grief had passed for that moment, replaced by the kind of peace and joy that only God can give. His Word proved true in the most unexpected place in the quiet aftermath of lament, under the steady hand of His comfort.

Say this out loud: **My joy comes in the morning.**

Now declare this: **I declare that sorrow is only temporary, but God's favor and joy remain with me for a lifetime.**

God's discipline and anger are brief, but His favor lasts forever. Seasons of weeping and hardship may come, yet they are not permanent. In Christ, we have the assurance that joy will return, just as surely as morning follows night. This verse encourages us to hold on through pain and grief, trusting that God's goodness and lasting favor will bring comfort, renewal, and hope.

Prayer of Reflection

Lord, You have been faithful to me in my deepest sorrow. When the waves of grief crashed over me and I felt I could not go on, You reminded me that weeping may endure for the night, but joy comes in the morning. In the darkness of my lament, You whispered hope into my spirit. Thank You for proving that Your Word is true—that sorrow is never the end of my story, because Your joy and Your favor remain forever. Teach me to trust You in the long nights of grief, and to look with expectation for the joy You promise with each new dawn. Amen.

O death, where is your victory? O death, where is your sting? Now sin is the sting of death, and sin exercises its power [upon the soul] through [the abuse of] the Law. But thanks be to God, Who gives us the victory [making us conquerors] through our Lord Jesus Christ. Therefore, my beloved brethren, be firm (steadfast), immovable, always abounding in the work of the Lord [always being superior, excelling, doing more than enough in the service of the Lord], knowing and being continually aware that your labor in the Lord is not futile [it is never wasted or to no purpose]. 1 Corinthians 15:55-58

I wasn't sure how I was supposed to claim victory in the middle of such crushing grief. The loss felt so final, so heavy, that victory seemed out of reach. Yet the words of Paul from 1 Corinthians 15 kept reverberating in my spirit: *"O death, where is your victory? O death, where is your sting?"*

Those words reminded me of a truth I desperately needed to cling to, that because of Jesus, death does not win. Even though I felt broken and alone, I had to put all my trust and faith in God and His Word. I realized that my calling in this season was not to understand all the "whys," but to remain firm and immovable in my faith, trusting that God was in control and surrendering to His plan for my life.

In the quiet moments of aloneness, the ache of loss threatened to consume me. But when I lifted my hands in praise, choosing to worship through the tears, I felt His presence with me. He was walking beside me in my grief, steadying my heart with His comfort.

It was then that I sensed a deeper purpose unfolding. I knew I needed to finish this devotional, not just for myself, but for the countless wives who had walked a similar path of caregiving, loss, and longing. My grief would not silence me; instead, it would become the soil where hope could grow for others.

In that moment, purpose began to replace despair. I found purpose in my aloneness, not because it was easy, but because it drove me deeper into the arms of God. I found purpose in resting in Him, letting His strength carry me where my own strength failed. My spirit kept whispering the truth: as long as I kept Him first in my life, all would be well.

Say this out loud: **Thanks be to God, who gives me the victory.**

Now declare this: **I declare that death has no victory and sin has no sting over me, for through Christ's triumph I stand firm, unshakable, and abounding in His work, knowing that my labor in the Lord is never in vain.**

The writings of Paul remind us that death does not have the final word, because Christ has overcome both sin and the grave. For those who mourn, this truth brings comfort. Our loved ones who believed in Him now share in His victory, and we, too, will one day experience the joy of eternal life. Until then, we can rest in the assurance that nothing done in the Lord is ever wasted, and that His hope carries us through our sorrow.

Prayer of Reflection

Lord, in the midst of my grief, I surrender to You. When the pain feels overwhelming and death seems to have stolen so much, remind me that in Christ, death has no victory and no lasting sting. Strengthen me to remain firm and unshakable in my faith, even when I feel weak. Take my aloneness and turn it into purpose. Use my story, my tears, and even my brokenness to bring encouragement to others who walk this same path. I place my future, my family, and my heart in Your hands. As long as I keep You first, I know all will be well, because You are with me. Amen.

My flesh and my heart may fail, but God is the Rock and firm Strength of my heart and my Portion forever. Psalm 73:26

Watching Doug take his last breath here on earth left me heartbroken in a way I could never have imagined. My strength failed me, and silent tears traced their way down my cheeks as I sat beside him. The hospice nurses leaned in close, listening for a heartbeat, searching for a pulse. Finally, they pronounced his passing at 10:33 a.m. on July 17, 2024.

I remember smiling through my tears when they asked for the time. Neither nurse wore a watch, nor did they have their phones nearby. It struck me as both tender and surreal that I was the one to provide the time of Doug's passing. I glanced down at my wrist, at the watch Doug had given me the year before, when we celebrated our 40th wedding anniversary. That gift, once just a marker of time shared together, became the very witness of the moment he stepped into eternity.

I knew the truth of Scripture, that to *be absent from the body is to be present with the Lord* (2 Corinthians 5:8). I clung to that knowledge, whispering it to myself as an anchor in the storm. But my heart and my flesh screamed at the injustice of it all. How could it be that at only 59 years old, I was now called "widow"? In an instant, my identity had shifted. The love of my life was gone from this earth, and the word I had dreaded became part of who I was.

In that moment, reality pressed down hard. I was alone. The weight of responsibility fell squarely on my shoulders. I was the one who had to make the phone calls. Our family and closest friends were scattered across Wyoming and other states. No one was nearby except my pastor, the only familiar face in the city where Doug and I lived.

I had no choice but to lean fully on God's strength. My own had completely run out. Somehow, I had to function. I had to take the next breath, make the next call, take the next step. I had to put one foot in front of the other and keep moving forward, even when every part of me wanted to collapse. I had to live.

And in that moment of breaking, God's presence surrounded me. His Spirit whispered to me that though my earthly companion was gone, I was not abandoned. I would walk a new path, one I had never wanted to take, but I would not walk it alone.

Say this out loud: **I stand firmly on the Rock Who is my Strength and my Portion.**

Now declare this: **I declare that even when my strength fails, God is my Strength and my Portion forever.**

The Psalmist Asaph reminds us that our human strength and even our hearts may fail, but God Himself is our everlasting strength and our eternal portion. He is the one we can depend on when everything else fades away.

Prayer of Reflection

Lord, my heart aches as I remember the moment when Doug took his last breath. The silence of that hour felt unbearable, and the weight of widowhood pressed upon me in an instant. Yet even in my weakness, You were there. Thank You for reminding me that to be absent from the body is to be present with You. Still, Father, You know how my heart and flesh cried out at the pain of that reality.

Give me strength when I have none of my own. Teach me to lean fully on You for every breath, every step, every decision. When I feel the crushing loneliness of doing life without Doug, surround me with Your presence and whisper Your peace to my soul. Help me to trust that even though my path has changed, I am not walking it alone. Be my strength, my comfort, and my portion forever. Amen.

In the Quiet Place: Pages of Hope and Healing

A Guided Space for Reflection and Renewal

When the Valley Feels Dark

Read: Psalm 23: 4

Even in the valley of the deepest sorrow, God does not abandon us. His presence walks beside us when the weight of caregiving feels unbearable. The darkness may surround, but His comfort remains a constant light – steady, sure, and tender.

Journal Prompts:

- What moments of fear or exhaustion have felt like "the valley" in your own journey?

- How has God comforted or carried you when you could not see the way forward?

- Write a declaration of faith that you will not walk alone that God's rod and staff still guide and protect you.

- *I was encouraged by...*

A Stength I Didn't Know I Had
Read: Deuteronomy 31:6

True courage isn't the absence of fear, it's trusting God in the middle of it. When everything seems uncertain, His promises to go before us steadies our trembling hearts and reminds us we are never forsaken.

Journal Prompts:

- When have you felt God strengthening you in ways you didn't expect?

- What fears do you need to surrender in His presence today?

- Write a personal declaration of courage rooted in God's promise to be with you.

- *I was encouraged by...*

Faith in the Furnace
Read: Daniel 3:17-18
Faith doesn't always remove us from the fire, sometimes it sustains us within it. God's power and presence become most real when we trust Him even if the outcome doesn't go our way.

Journal Prompts:
- What fires have tested your faith during caregiving or grief?

- How has God revealed Himself to you in the middle of those trials?

- Write a declaration of trust: even if the outcome is uncertain, you will still praise Him.

- *I was encouraged by...*

The Weight of Waiting
Read: Psalm 27:14

Waiting isn't wasted when God is in it. In the stillness of waiting room and unanswered prayers, He strengthens our hearts and teaches us endurance through trust.

Journal Prompts:

- How do you handle seasons of waiting when you long for answers?

- What has God taught you about patience in your caregiving or grief journey?

- Write a prayer asking God to strengthen you as you wait with faith and hope.

- *I wasn encouraged by...*

Anchored by Grace
Read: Ephesians 2:8

Grace is a steady anchor in the storm. It reminds us that God's favor cannot be earned — it is freely given, even when we feel we've failed. His grace holds us when our strength runs out.

Journal Prompts:

- When have you tried to "earn" God's favor through striving or perfection?

- What does His free gift of grace mean to you in this season?

- Write a declaration reminding yourself that you are sustained by grace, and not by effort.

- *I am encouraged by...*

Courage in the Breaking
Read: 2 Corinthians 12:9

God's strength is made perfect in weakness. The cracks of our hearts become the very places where His light shines through most brightly.

Journal Prompts:

- How has your weakness become a place for God's strength to show up?

- What broken pieces is God asking you to surrender to His healing today?

- Write a declaration of faith: "Your grace is sufficient for me, Lord."

- *I am encouraged by...*

Unseen but Steady
Read: 2 Corinthians 5:7

Faith is believing what we cannot see and walking forward in trust when the outcome is hidden. We learn to see with eternal eyes to recognize that God's unseen hand is guiding every step.

Journal Prompts:

- What situation are you facing right now that requires unseen faith?

- How can you remind yourself daily that God is working, even when you can't see it?

- Write a declaration affrming that your faith, not sight, will lead your steps.

- *I am encouraged by...*

When Words Bring Life
Read: Proverbs 18:21

Our words create the atmosphere we live in. Life and death truly are in the power of the tongue. In caregiving, our speech can either lift or crush our own hearts. Speaking life builds faith, peace, and hope even in dark circumstances.

Journal Prompts:

- What kind of words do you tend to speak over yourself and your situation?

- How can you replace fear-based words with life-giving declarations?

- Write a short declaration that you will speak over your day.

- *I was encouraged by...*

The Gift of Surrender
Read: Romans 5:15

Grace is the gift that replaces our striving. When we finally lay down the need to control outcomes and fix everything ourselves, we make room for the abundant grace of Christ to flow through our weaknesses.

Journal Prompts:

- In what areas of caregiving or grief do you struggles to surrender control?

- How has God's grace shown up for you when you finally let go?

- Write a prayer of surrender — release every "what if" into His hands.

- *I was encouraged by...*

The God Who Heals
Read: Jeremiah 17:14

Healing comes in many forms — sometimes in the body, sometimes in the heart, and always in the spirit. God binds our wounds and restores our hope, often in ways we don't expect.

Journal Prompts:

- What kind of healing are you asking God for today — physical, emotional, spiritual?

- Where have you already seen glimpses of His restoration in your story?

- Write a declaration of faith that healing is still possible with God.

- *I was encouraged by...*

Grace to Keep Going
Read: Isaiah 41:10

When fear threatens to overtake us, God whispers, "Do not be afraid." His promise to strengthen, help, and uphold us becomes the lifeline that keeps us standing when we feel like falling.

Journal Prompts:

- What fears have gripped your heart during this season?

- How has God's strength helped you continue when you wanted to give up?

- Write a prayer thanking God for upholding you when you felt weak.

- *I was encouraged by...*

His Glory in Our Grief
Read: Isaiah 60:1

Even in grief, God calls us to arise and shine. His glory covers our brokenness with divine light, reminding us that beauty and purpose can still bloom in the ashes.

Journal Prompts:

- What does it mean for you to "arise" in this current season?

- How has God revealed His light in your dark moments?

- Write a declaration of renewal: "Your glory still rises in me, Lord."

- *I was encouraged by...*

The Comfort of His Presence
Read: Psalm 34:18

God draws near to the brokenhearted. He never rushes our healing or ignores our pain. In the tender stillness of His presence, our mourning turns to comfort, and our sorrow finds peace.

Journal Prompts:

- How have you experienced God's nearness in your grief?

- What small comforts has He provided that remind you you're not alone?

- Write a prayer of gratitude for His presence in your broken places.

- *I was encouraged by...*

When Faith Feels Small
Read: Hebrews 11:6

Faith pleases God not because it's big or bold, but because it's real. Even mustard seed faith delights His heart. When we come to Him honestly — scared, tired, uncertain — He rewards our seeking with His steady presence.

Journal Prompts:

- When has your faith felt small but steady?

- How can you nurture your faith when your strength is fading?

- Write a declaration: "Even in my smallest faith, I wil still seek You."

- *I'm encouraged by...*

Peace Beyond Fear

Read: 1 Peter 3:14

The world tells us to fear but God's Word tells us to be unshaken. When we place our confidence in Him, no diagnosis, opinion, or outcome can take our peace.

Journal Prompts:

- What fears have tried to steal your peace?

- How can you protect your heart from words or reports that stir anxiety?

- Write a declaration of peace anchored in God's promises.

- *I was encouraged by...*

The Gift of a United Heart
Read: Ephesians 4:26-27

Anger is a natural response to pain but unresloved anger can create cracks in the foundation of love. God calls us to address our anger with honesty, humility, and forgiveness, refusing to give the enemy a foothold.

Journal Prompts:

- What unresolved emotions might be keeping you from peace?

- How can you express anger in ways that lead to healing instead of harm?

- Write a prayer inviting God to soften your heart and restore unity in your relationships.

- *I was encouraged by...*

Hope in the Middle of the Storm
Read: Romans 15:13

True hope isn't built on outcomes — it's anchored in the unchanging nature of God. When our hearts are full of fear and uncertainty, His Spirit fills us with joy and peace so that we overflow with hope, even in the storm.

Journal Prompts:

- What does hope look like to you right now?

- How has God given you glimpses of joy in the middle of pain?

- Write a declaration: "My hope is anchored in You, Lord, not in what I see."

- *I was encouraged by...*

When Fear Feeds on the Future
Read: Proverbs 29:25

The fear of people and circumstances can feel like a snare, but trust in the Lord brings safety. Cancer, uncertainty, and loss whisper threats yet God reminds us that His presence is our refuge, and His faithfulness is our protection.

Journal Prompts:

- What fears about the future have tried to hold you captive?

- How has trusting God changed the way you see your circumstances?

- Write a prayer surrendering every "what if" to His perfect care.

- *I was encouraged by...*

When God Feels Silent
Read: Psalm 147:3

When it feels like God is quiet, He is often healing. In the silence of heartbreak and exhaustion, He gently binds up our wounds and restores our souls in ways we can't yet see.

Journal Prompts:

- How has God met you in the quiet places of grief or waiting?

- What wounds are you asking Him to bind up today?

- Write a declaration of trust in His unseen work of healing.

- *I was encouraged by...*

Walking Each Day by Faith
Read: 2 Corinthians 5:7

To walk by faith means choosing to trust God when we can't see the outcome. Faith becomes our steady rhythm — one step, one prayer, one breath at a time — until we find ourselves standing in His peace.

Journal Prompts:

- What does walking by faith look like for you today?

- In what area do you need to trust God with your next step?

- Write a declaration of confidence: "I walk by faith, not by sight."

- *I was encouraged by...*

The Faith That Works
Read: James 2:17
Faith without action is lifeless, but when we act on what we believe, faith becomes alive and transformative. Even the smallest act of obedience, done in love, bears fruit in the hardest seasons.

Journal Prompts:
- How can you put your faith into action this week?

- What small step of obedience is God calling you to take?

- Write a declaration: "My faith will live through my actions."

- *I was encouraged by...*

Strengthened in Suffering
Read: 2 Chronicles 32:7-8

God strengthens our hearts in battle, reminding us that those who are with us are geater than those against us. Even in suffering, He equips us with courage that comes not from might, but from faith.

Journal Prompts:

- When have you felt God's strength in your weakest moments?

- How can you remind yourself daily that God fights for you?

- Write a prayer of courage, trusting that He will uphold you.

- *I was encouraged by...*

Healing in His Time
Read: Jeremiah 30:17

God promises to restore health and heal wounds. Healing may not come as we expect, but His restoration reaches deeper than the body — into the soul that aches and the heart that has been torn.

Journal Prompts:

- Where do you need God's healing most right now?

- How have you seen glimpses of His restoration in your journey?

- Write a prayer thanking Him for His promises to restore.

- *I was encouraged by...*

Resting in His Care
Read: 1 Peter 5:6-7

When the weight of caregiving and grief feels unbearable, God invites us to cast every care on Him. He does not watch from a distance. He cares personally, tenderly, and completely for us.

Journal Prompts:

- What burdens do you need to release into God's hands today?

- How does knowing he cares "watchfully" change your perspective?

- Write a prayer of surrender, resting in His gentle care.

- *I was encouraged by...*

The God Who Restores
Read: Psalm 30:2

God not only hears our cries for healing, He responds with compassion. His restoration reaches beyond what is broken to renew the strength, peace, and purpose within us.

Journal Prompts:

- How has God brought healing to your body, heart, or spirit?

- What does "restoration" mean to you in this season of life?

- Write a prayer thanking Him for hearing your cry and answering with mercy.

- *I was encouraged by...*

Joy in the Morning
Read: Psalm 30:5

Grief may linger for the night, but joy always greets you in the morning. God's faithfulness ensures that no sorrow lasts forever. His light always breaks through the darkness.

Journal Prompts:

- When have you experienced God turning your mourning into joy?

- How can you look for glimpses of joy even in your waiting?

- Write a declaration: "My joy will rise again in the morning."

- *I was encouraged by...*

The Gift of Godly Sorrow
Read: 2 Corinthians 7:6

Not all sorrow is destructive. Godly sorrow leads to repentance, restoration, and renewal. It draws us closer to God, reminding us that even our tears have purpose.

Journal Prompts:

- What emotions have you struggled to surrender to God?

- How has grief refined or deepened your faith?

- Write a prayer inviting God to transform your sorrow into strength.

- *I was encouraged by...*

Faith Over Feelings
Read: 1 Corinthians 16:13

When emotions overwhelm, faith steadies us. Standing firm in Christ doesn't mean we never feel afraid or weary. It means we keep our eyes on the One who never changes.

Journal Prompts:

- How has faith helped you to stand when your emotions were unstable?

- What truths from Scripture strengthen you when you feel weak?

- Write a declaration of courage: "I will stand firm in faith."

- *I was encouraged by...*

Covered by His Glory
Read: Psalm 84:11

God withholds no good thing from those who walk uprightly. Even in hardship, His grace and glory cover us like a shield, sustaining us through what we cannot control.

Journal Prompts:

- Where have you seen God's goodness in unexpected places?

- What good thing are you believing God to reveal in His timing?

- Write a prayer of gratitude for His covering grace.

- *I was encouraged by...*

Faith That Overcomes Fear
Read: Matthew 14:27

When Jesus says, "Take courage; it is I. Do not be afraid," fear loses its hold. His voice cuts through the storm and reminds us that peace is not the absence of chaos but the presence of Christ.

Journal Prompts:

- What storms have you faced that required you to trust His voice?

- How can you choose courage when fear threatens your peace?

- Write a declaration of faith: "I will not fear, for You are with me."

- *I was encouraged by...*

Rooted in Hope
Read: Romans 12:12

Hope anchors our hearts in the middle of hardship. Through patient endurance and constant prayer, we are strengthened to rejoice even when the outcome is unknown.

Journal Prompts:

- What keeps your hope alive when life feels uncertain?

- How can you cultivate joy in your current circumstances?

- Write a prayer asking God to renew your hope today.

- *I was encouraged by...*

Grace in the Humbling

Read: James 4:6

God gives grace to the humble — those who admit their need for Him. When we stop trying to be strong on our own, His power gently fills the spaces where our strength ends.

Journal Prompts:

- What situations have reminded you of your dependence on God?

- How has humility opened the door for His grace in your life?

- Write a prayer of surrender, thanking God for meeting you in humility.

- *I was encouraged by...*

The Steadfast Heart
Read: Psalm 112:7-8

Faith steadies the heart when bad news comes. The believer's confidence is not rooted in outcomes but in the unshakable character of God, whose promises never fail.

Journal Prompts:

- When have you had to trust God despite difficult news?

- How can you strengthen your heart to remain steady in faith?

- Write a declaration of trust: "My heart is fixed, steadfast in You."

- *I was encouraged by...*

The Beauty of Believing Again
Read: 3 John 2

God desires that our souls prosper; that our inner life be whole, healed, and at peace. As our souls flourish, our hearts and minds align with His abundant care.

Journal Prompts:

- How is your soul prospering today?

- What would "wholeness" look like for you in this season?

- Write a prayer of renewal, asking God to restore peace and vitatlity to your soul.

- *I was encouraged by...*

Arise in the Light of His Love
Read: Psalm 91:14-16

When we set our love upon the Lord, He promises deliverance, protection, and long life. His love becomes the dwelling place where fear cannot stay and faith can grow.

Journal Prompts:

- How can you more intentionally "set your love" upon the Lord this week?

- Where has He shown you His faithfulness in protection or peace?

- Write a declaration: "Because I love You, I will trust You, Lord."

- *I was encouraged by...*

Afterword — A Letter from My Heart

Dear Friend,

As you close this book, I pray you feel seen, strengthened, and surrounded by the love of God. Whether you are in the midst of caregiving, standing in the valley of grief, or finding your way toward healing, please know — **you are not alone**.

I have walked through the same long nights of uncertainty and the same mornings where faith was my only strength. Through every moment, I have found one unshakable truth: **God is faithful.** He never left my side, even when I didn't know what to pray. He carried me when my own strength failed, and He filled my empty places with His peace.

The same God who comforted me wants to comfort you. He loves you more deeply than words can describe and longs to walk with you through every season of your life — in the hospital rooms, in the quiet spaces, and in the moments you can't see the way forward.

If you do not know Jesus as your Savior and Lord, I invite you to receive Him now. He is your Peace, your Healer, and your Hope. Simply pray this prayer in faith, and Jesus will be your Lord:

Heavenly Father, I admit that I have sinned. I repent. I believe in my heart that You raised Jesus from the dead. I confess with my mouth, Jesus is Lord and my Savior. Right now, I receive forgiveness. By the Blood of Jesus, I am saved. In Jesus' Name. Amen.

If you prayed that prayer, welcome to the family of God. You are no longer alone, the Lord Himself is walking beside you, giving you strength, hope, and new life.

Hold fast to His promises. Rest in His love. And remember — even here, even now, **everything is going to be all right.**

With love and grace,

Alisa Cochrane
Preacher's Hill Publishing
www.alisacochrane.com

Acknowlegments

This book could not have come to life without the encouragement, prayers, and wisdom of the many people who walked beside me through its creation.

To my dear friends and peers at Kingdom Creative Writers and Casper Writers thank you for your fellowship, insight, and faith. You reminded me that writing is not a solitary act, but a sacred partnership between the heart, the page, and the people who believe in the message.

A special thank you to Leslie, Neva, Patti, Cari, Deb, Marian, Mary Beth and Wes. Your gentle honesty, keen eyes, and unwavering belief in this project helped me see both the flaws and the beauty of what God was shaping through these words. You each spoke truth in love, and because of that, this work is stronger, deeper, and more faithful to its purpose.

To every writer, reader, and encourager who reminded me to press on when the words came slowly and the memories felt heavy—thank you. You helped birth this story into the world.

And above all, I give thanks to my Lord and Savior, Jesus Christ, who turned my grief into purpose and my sorrow into song.

"Those who sow in tears shall reap with shouts of joy."—*Psalm 126:5*

About the Author

Alisa Cochrane is an author and kingdom creative entrepreneur who enjoys writing books that encourage women in the midst of their greatest challenges. Widowed in 2024, Alisa was her husband Doug's primary caregiver during his battle against lung cancer. A follower of Jesus, Alisa is the mother of three children and grandmother to eight. She lives in the big, beautiful state of Wyoming.

If this book has encouraged you, I would love to hear from you. Your story matters, and it is a privilege to walk beside you on this sacred journey of faith and healing.

To share your testimony, ask questions, or learn more about upcoming projects, you may reach me directly at:

Email: alisa@alisacochrane.com

Let's continue walking together—one prayer, one page, and one promise at a time.

Learn more about Alisa and Preacher's Hill Publishing at www.alisacochrane.com

Scripture References

HOPE
Romans 12:12
Psalm 33:18
1 Timothy 4:10
Romans 15:4
Romans 15:13
Lamentations 3:24-26

FAITH
Romans 3:28
Mark 11:23-25
James 2:17
2 Corinthians 5:7
Hebrews 11:6

DEPRESSION
Deuteronomy 31:8
1 Peter 5:6-7
Isaiah 60:1
2 Corinthians 7:6
Psalm 91:14-16

GRACE
Psalm 84:11
James 4:6
Ephesians 2:8
Romans 5:15

FEAR AND DESPAIR
Psalm 23:4
1 John 4:18
1 Peter 3:14
Isaiah 41:10
Proverbs 29:25
Psalm 112:7-8
Ephesians 4:26-27

COURAGE
1 John 5:14
Deuteronomy 31:6
2 Chronicles 32:7-8
1 Corinthians 16:13
Matthew 14:27
Psalm 27:14

HEALTH AND HEALING
Psalm 30:2
3 John 2
Jeremiah 17:14
James 5:14-15
Psalm 147:3
Jeremiah 30:17

GRIEF
John 11:25
Matthew 5:14
Psalm 34:18
Psalm 30:5
1 Corinthians 15:55-58
Psalm 73:26

NOTES

www.ingramcontent.com/pod-product-compliance
Lightning Source LLC
Chambersburg PA
CBHW020246130626
46549CB00005B/2093